PARADISE

Stories of a Changing Chesapeake

by J. H. Hall

Rappahannock Press, Inc.

Library of Congress Catalogue Card Number
94-69193

International Standard Book Number
1-880902-07-9

First Edition, 1994. Second Edition, 1995.

Published in the United States of America
by
Rappahannock Press, Inc.
276 Virginia Street, P.O. Box 549
Urbanna, VA 23175

Contents

Bird Hunting As It Used To Be And Still Is   1
Paradise   12
Mates For Life   27
Pilgrims   40
Russian Agents On The Chesapeake Bay   53
One That Got Away   65
Otha's Ghost   77
Parable   90
Close To Nature   102
Arrowheads   114

All characters and incidents in this book are fictional.

"Bird Hunting As It Used To Be And Still Is" and "Russian Agents On The Chesapeake Bay" were printed in slightly different form in Gray's Sporting Journal. "Mates for Life" was printed in Shooting Sportsman.

Illustrations: Copyright © by Bill Martz, Star Route Box 565, Lottsburg, VA 22511. Used by permission.

About the illustrations:

For 16 years, the work of artist Bill Martz has been referred to as "…a love affair with Virginia and the Northern Neck." A native of Maryland, his home studio is in the Lewisetta area of Northumberland County, where he creates in pen and ink, watercolor, acrylics and oils. His work is found in private and corporate collections throughout the country. His company, Bill Martz Impressions, distributes notepaper, prints and designer sportswear reflecting the essence of the Chesapeake Bay area.

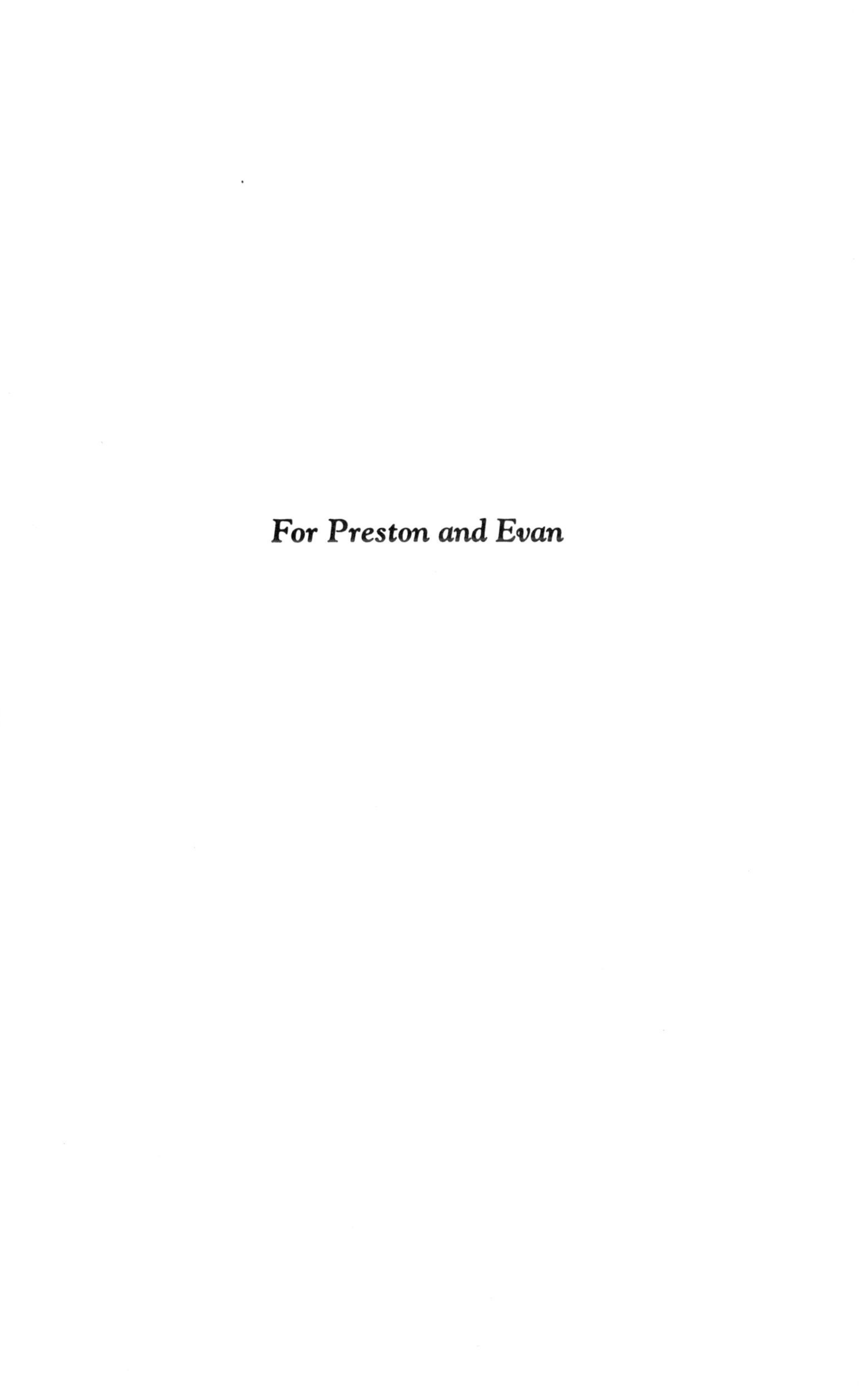

For Preston and Evan

Bird Hunting As It Used To Be And Still Is

Lester Harmon was a bird hunter. As a rule he didn't shoot squirrels, but he was seriously considering making an exception for the one now sassing his bird dog, Sarge, from the safety of a large red oak in Sam and Elsie Harmon's yard. "You're just lucky there's a car in the drive," Lester said. "That's all I've got to say." The squirrel flattened itself like a throw rug against the furrowed bark. Its tail twitched like a windup toy's.

Usually if Sarge chased a squirrel, Lester would shout at him, sometimes even take a shot, because

Sarge was a bird dog, a pointer. He wasn't supposed to chase squirrels. But this squirrel, before Sarge ran him up a tree, had been feeding where they used to find birds — quail! At one time the place had been a farm, with fields of soybeans, wide hedgerows, and heavily wooded points. Three related families had been raised on that farm. Everyone but Lester moved away. Later they returned, cleared the points, built houses, planted grass, and — the final insult — erected bird feeders. Sam's and Elsie's was a plastic, mushroom-shaped contraption suspended from a metal post. The post was set in concrete; it was permanent, like a monument. A memorial was how Lester saw it, a grave marker.

Now where quail once roosted, songbirds the size of pullets fattened on sunflower seeds, and grey squirrels feeding on the spillage grew as large as young groundhogs. It bothered Lester, this desecration. It played on his mind.

The squirrel started up again. "Shut up, fatso," Lester said. It was quiet for a minute. Then a songbird chirped from a nearby tree. "You shut up too," Lester said. As far as Lester was concerned, the only bird song worth singing was "bob-white." If a songbird couldn't sing "bob-white," it ought to keep its mouth shut.

A window opened, and Elsie Harmon's voice came blasting through. "Get on away from there, you nasty thing," she shouted at Sarge. "Go on! Shoo!"

"It's all right," Lester shouted. "I'll take care of it."

"Oh, Lester, I didn't see you," Elsie said.

"Just taking the dog out for a little exercise."

"All right. If you can keep him away from the azaleas, that would be nice."

"I don't think he's hurt'em. He's got bigger things on his mind. Now come on, Sarge, leave that squirrel alone."

As Sarge moved slowly from the yard, the squirrel cut loose with another barrage of belligerent chatter, as if he personally had run Sarge off. "Fatso," Lester said, "you had better watch your mouth. I mean it." The window slammed shut. He hoped Elsie, who was a little overweight, didn't think he was talking to her.

"See what you got us into," Lester yelled at Sarge, as the dog bounded across the dirt road and raced out into a bare stubble field. "I told you it wouldn't be any good."

On the other hand, Elsie shouldn't have called Sarge "nasty," even if there was a little truth in it. He wasn't really nasty; he just had the disposition of a hunting dog, not a pet, and if you weren't someone who took him hunting, he didn't have much use for you. Lately, since Lester hadn't hunted him for over three years, the dog hadn't had much use for Lester. The feeling was mutual.

"I wish you could see how foolish you look running around in a bare stubble field," Lester said. The dog had his nose low to the ground, as if he might actually find birds where there wasn't cover.

At times Lester had had good hunting in that field, at first with his father, then alone, then with his nephew, Roy, then alone again. The first bird Roy ever killed came from that field. Sarge — he was just a pup then — started the covey in the edge of the soybeans. The birds ran; he trailed them into the hedgerow. Some short-haired dogs would have stayed on the edge and pointed, but Sarge burrowed through the brush after them. His tail turned red from the briers. He trailed the birds to the marsh where the field met Muddy Creek. The entire covey flushed wild out of range and flew across the creek to the beach. The birds wouldn't run across the bare sand. They held until, one by one, Sarge pointed them and Lester kicked them up. Four straight times Roy missed. On the fifth bird, he broke a wing. Sarge pounced on the cripple, crunched it once in his jaws and started to swallow. Then Roy pounced on Sarge. He straddled the dog's back and pushed his top lip into his canine teeth until his mouth opened. Then Roy rammed his free hand halfway down the dog's throat, extracted the bird and held it up just as proudly as if the bird had still had feathers.

"Still be good eating," Roy said.

"Darn right it will."

That was back when they left a few rows of beans along the edges for the birds. Now the field was farmed clean. Now if a bean did fall to the ground, unless a crow found it, it lay there until it rotted.

Lester followed the dirt road to where it crossed the tarred road in to town and became a tunnel through hardwood and pine. The light formed a calico pattern on the red dirt. Sarge ran through the woods, visible now and then as a flash of white, then sinking back into the trees. Lester could follow the rise and fall of the dog's excitement through the rhythm of his footsteps on the dry forest floor. He hoped the exercise would settle the dog; Sarge had been so restless. It was something about the time of year, the cool air,

4

the lower angle of the sun, the leathery smell of the fallen leaves. Lester could feel it too, but what could he do about it now that the hunting was over? Every fall since the hunting ended he had the same tug of war with his dog. The only difference this year was, the dog won.

Sarge waited in a gravel drive that would have led to the sedge field had it still existed, but which now led to another new house. "Well," Lester said, when he reached the dog, "you wanted to hunt, so hunt." Sarge charged up the drive, then cut out into the yard, his nose held high, winding. Lester stood in the yard and watched, but what he saw was a younger Sarge bounding deer-like through a field thick with sedge grass, scrub pine, and briers, and behind the dog, a younger, more alert Lester, his gun held lightly in both hands, ready. The day the bulldozer arrived at the sedge field was the day Lester put his bird gun away — for good, he'd thought at the time.

He'd heard the big diesel from his bedroom window and walked with his gun and dog to investigate. He stood where he was standing now and watched as the machine made one pass after another across the field, carrying sedge grass, small trees, vines — parts of him it felt like — ahead of it. And the whole time that was happening Sarge was running around in front of the bulldozer, hunting. As his territory was being rolled up behind him like a carpet, Sarge kept looking in what was left of it for birds. He found a covey too, and pointed them and waited, but Lester was afraid to shoot for fear of hitting the dozer operator, though at the time he felt more like shooting him than the birds. At least he had until the fellow

—it was just a kid—climbed down out of the driver's seat and came over and asked Lester for a cigarette, and Lester recognized him. It was Clinton Lee, C.E. Lee's oldest boy by his first marriage.

So while the diesel idled in the background, Lester and Clinton Lee stood in the warm November sun and smoked cigarettes and talked of fish and crabs and oysters, and Lester's anger collapsed around him like a tent, and turned into something else, something worse. He didn't know exactly what to call it, but he felt it now as he watched this dumb, noble dog of his search for quail in a concrete garage and lift his leg to car tires and azaleas, as if with his urine he could turn back the clock and reclaim his old territory. "Come on, Sarge," Lester shouted. "We're going home." But Sarge was still busy in the garage and ignored Lester. "To hell with you then," Lester said. "I'm going home."

Lester started up the road. Soon Sarge came barreling up behind him, roughly brushing his leg as he passed. "Why don't you watch where you're going!" Lester said, as the dog darted off into the woods. Sarge's attitude was starting to get to him, the way the dog acted like they were still hunting just as they had always hunted, and nope, they hadn't found any birds in that yard or that garage, but maybe they would in the next. "You're a fool," Lester yelled. "You're the worst kind of fool there is."

They were nice people that moved into the house in the sedge field, and nice people, too, that moved onto the orchard point, and more nice people that moved into the four other new houses on that farm. They were Harmons; they were family, and he loved them just as they loved him, but they couldn't have done a better job of ruining the bird hunting on that farm if they had tried, and all the sunflower seeds in the world wouldn't bring it back, because quail were strange creatures. You could shoot a covey down almost to its last pair, and next fall that covey would be back bigger than ever, but if you tampered with its territory, if you destroyed its roosting place, that covey would disappear. You couldn't crowd two coveys into the space of one either. Quail needed room, more room than you could explain by their need for anything, except their need for room. Lester couldn't really explain it, but he sort of understood it.

On the way home he killed the squirrel. It wasn't planned; it just happened. He hadn't even been thinking about that squirrel. He was just walking up the road minding his own business, and when he passed Sam and Elsie's place, the squirrel, which was feeding in the yard, sat up and said something. To Lester it sounded like some kind of wise crack. When Lester moved closer so he could hear better, the squirrel ignored him. It just dropped back down and started feeding as if Lester wasn't any threat at all, as if he didn't even exist. It was the closest Lester had ever seen an animal come to suicide. Even then it wasn't easy.

First he had to get in range. A squirrel, even a fat, loudmouthed squirrel, won't let you walk right up to him. And there wasn't any cover. But the car was gone, and that meant Sam and Elsie had gone to town, if one went, they both went. They did everything together. The way they drove, town was twenty minutes one way. So Lester knew he had time. He approached slowly, moving only when the squirrel fed, always stopping in the same position just before the squirrel sat up. From the squirrel's perspective, all that changed was Lester's size; he was slowly growing larger. If the squirrel ever noticed, he never put two and two together.

If Lester got caught, he had an alibi: he was shooting mistletoe for the relatives. He was going to give them each a sprig of mistletoe for Christmas, decorated with a red ribbon. The squirrel got caught in the line of fire. It happened.

The songbirds that had been swarming around the feeder like bees almost gave Lester away. When he got in gun range, they grew very quiet, then one by one flitted off into the trees. The squirrel sat up and looked around longer than usual, but was glassy-eyed and lethargic. When the squirrel dropped back down onto all fours, Lester raised his gun, took careful aim, and then Sarge came charging across the yard and chased the squirrel back up the red oak. "Darn fool dog," Lester said.

The squirrel was halfway up the trunk, facing down, yapping at Sarge. Before Lester could get off a shot, the squirrel darted around to the other side of the tree. "I guess he's not as tame as I thought," Lester said.

Sarge ran around to the other side, but the squirrel would not be chased back to Lester. Cautiously Lester circled the tree, but when he got to the other side all he saw was a bushy tail disappearing around the horizon of trunk. He found a large stone and slung it up into the branches on the far side. It crashed loudly to the ground, but the squirrel stayed put. Then he threw a branch, again to no avail. The squirrel started chattering again. To Lester it sounded like laughter.

"You still haven't caught on, have you fatso?" Lester said. "You think this is some kind of game, don't you. Like tag or hide and seek." Lester rattled a rock off the branches near the squirrel. "A wild thing like you, mingling with songbirds, living on handouts. You ought to be ashamed of yourself. I'm ashamed of you. Aren't you, Sarge?" Sarge whined and scratched at the bark.

Lester started circling the tree, slowly at first, then faster and faster, waiting for the squirrel to mistime its movements. Soon he was walking full speed; he was almost running. Still he could not get a clear shot. Lester was soon tired and out of breath and had to sit down on a stump at the edge of the woods. As Lester pulled out his pack of Salems, he watched for the squirrel out of the corner of his eye. "I smoke too many of these," Lester said. "That's probably why I'm short of breath." He patted his stomach. "I eat too much too." He wasn't sleeping so well either. Some mornings he'd wake up early to the sound of quail whistling, but when he'd get to the window, all he would hear would be the chirping of the songbirds in the silver maples. It was hard to get back to sleep after that.

When Lester leaned forward to shield his cigarette lighter from the breeze, the squirrel made a run for it. He dashed out a long branch and leaped towards the outstretched limb of another tree that would have led to safety had Lester not raised his gun and shot the squirrel out of the air. The squirrel tumbled end over end, then crashed into a pile of dried leaves. "You made a better squirrel than you did a bird," Lester said, laying his gun back across his lap.

Soon he rubbed his cigarette out against the side of the stump and ejected the spent shell from his gun. He'd forgotten how sweet the smell of burnt gunpowder was. It was like the perfume of an old girlfriend. He placed the spent shell into the pocket of his hunting coat and walked over to get the squirrel.

Sarge was playing with the dead squirrel the way a cat plays with a mouse. "Give it here," Lester said. "Drop it. Drop!" Sarge stopped playing and held the squirrel tightly in his mouth. He glared up at Lester. The muscles along his liver and white flanks tensed. Lester's hands still bore scars from times he had tried to take birds before Sarge was ready to release them. You could only get away with that when you were young and didn't know the dangers. He went and found a large pine branch. He touched it lightly to Sarge's haunches, as if taking aim. Sarge flinched and dropped the squirrel. He had his scars too. "Come on, Boy," Lester said. "We're going home."

They walked side by side up the road to the house. Lester liked the feel of the squirrel in his game bag. It felt like three quail, two he'd taken on a covey rise, the third, a single bird that Sarge had worked perfectly, pointed and held until the bird flushed in a blur of wingbeats, then slowly came into focus and fell, streaming feathers like smoke, without a shot being fired, as if all Lester had to do to bring it down was see it clearly. Before Lester went inside, he took the spent shell and slung it as far out into the creek as he could, then stood and watched until the last ripple disappeared.

Lester sat in a chair in the entryway and unlaced his boots. When Sarge came over to get his head scratched, he had the same dopey, satisfied look on his face as when they had found four or five coveys and killed a limit. "What're you looking like that for?" Lester said. "Don't you know anything? Or you just don't care, is that it?" Sarge moaned as Lester dug in behind the ears. "Birds, squirrels — doesn't matter to you, does it? Bean fields, garages — it's all the same, isn't it?" Lester stopped scratching and looked deep back into the dog's eyes as if expecting a response. Nothing. Sarge pulled away, meandered over to his dog bowl, then collapsed into his bed and fell asleep. "What am I going to do with you?" Lester said. "What am I going to do?" Sarge whimpered, and his feet twitched in his sleep, as if in pursuit.

Lester removed the squirrel from his game bag and carried it into the kitchen. He skinned and cleaned it. He cut it into pieces and parboiled it for an hour in lightly salted water. Next he placed the pieces in a large frying pan with a little water, red cooking wine, a lot of black pepper and other spices. He filled the rest of the pan with cut up carrots, potatoes, and onions. Finally he simmered the whole works on top of the stove for another hour. It filled the kitchen with a strange, exotic aroma, like wild duck, but a little milder.

When it was done, he placed it all on a large platter and sat down and looked at his meal, the first squirrel ever cooked in that house. It didn't look bad. He poked at it with a fork. It looked O.K. It looked fine. But all he could eat were the vegetables.

Paradise

At first light Roy Simon was already up and on his way to his uncle's house. If you were going to be a commercial fisherman, you had to get up early. You couldn't lie around in bed all day like some people he knew.

The dirt road passed like a valley between two fields of corn. The stalks, some twice as tall as Roy, rustled in the light breeze. A quail whistled from the hedgerow. Roy whistled back, off-key, silencing the quail. "Awright," Roy said. "If that's how you're going to be, I'll see you in November." His family would be back for Thanksgiving, and he and his uncle, Lester

Harmon, would hunt birds together. Then at Christmas they would hunt ducks and geese. His father didn't hunt or fish. He sold real estate and played golf.

Last night there had been an argument about golf. It was a short argument. Roy didn't even like his father to bring his golf clubs to the country, but his father liked to practice sand irons on the bayshore. The bayshore was a sanctuary, wild, with no houses. You could walk for two miles and see nothing but washed up bottles, crab pot buoys and arrowheads. Once Roy had his picture in the Richmond Times with his arrowhead collection. He had tried to teach his father the names of the arrowheads — Halifax, Lamoka, Morrow Mountain — but it was hopeless. How could you teach something like that to a person who saw the bayshore as a big sand trap?

Lester lived alone on a narrow peninsula in a white frame house flanked by a pair of silver maples, whose limbs overhung the tin roof like protective arms. Roy stood in the yard and looked around at the cove and the crab floats; at Lester's dock and big boat, the Mary V.; at the white skiffs lying still in the water; and to the east at the creek and the beach and beyond the beach out into the bay, which seemed vast and endless. "This place *is* paradise," Roy said. "Why can't *he* see it?" Sometimes his father would walk around the place, using his hands as a viewfinder. Roy knew exactly what he was doing. He was measuring house lots.

Roy heard a noise, turned and saw his father's Buick station wagon pull into the yard. His father, Rud, was a large man with pinkish skin that wouldn't tan and thinning silvery hair. He walked over to Roy. "I'm still not playing golf," Roy said.

"You made that clear last night," his father said. His father looked around, his eyes adjusting to the dim light. "So," he said, "I thought, if you didn't mind, and if it was all right with Lester, I would go out fishing with you. With Lester."

"Oh," Roy said.

"If you don't think Lester would mind."

"No. No, I'm sure he wouldn't mind."

They walked down to the dock. Roy's father was wearing white Bermuda shorts, a baby blue golf shirt, and a pair of dark glasses dangling from his neck. Roy was wearing blue jeans, a tee shirt and tennis shoes. No dark glasses for Roy. Dark glasses were for city people, "come-hithers." Watermen, like Lester, didn't wear dark glasses; they wore baseball caps, and they squinted. Squinting was what caused the creases in the corners of their eyes that turned white when their faces relaxed. Lester's face was lined and furrowed like soft leather, like Roy's baseball glove. Otha's face was black and round as a catcher's mitt. Otha had worked for Lester longer than Roy had been alive.

He was loading boxes and barrels into the bow of the Mary V. when Roy and his father walked out onto the dock. Lester was tinkering with the engine. They were both wearing olive green oilskins and baseball caps. "Uh oh, Cap'n," Otha said, when he saw who was coming, "looks like we got a full crew today."

Lester looked up from the engine box. "Darned if we don't."

"I won't be in your way, will I?" Rud asked.

"No, indeed," Lester said. "Glad to have you. Can't pay much, though."

Roy laughed.

"He's telling the truth now," Otha said. "He don't pay anybody much."

"That's the trouble with people these days," Lester said. "They all want to make big money, but they don't want to work." Lester hit the ignition, and Otha's comeback was lost in the roar of the engine. Roy laughed anyway. He was sure that whatever Otha said would have been funny. He thought Otha and Lester were two of the most comical men he had ever known. He thought they should have been on TV.

"They're right funny, aren't they?" Roy said to his father. He had to shout to be heard over the engine.

His father nodded and patted his shirt pocket. "I wish I'd thought to bring my Dramamine," he said.

"What?"

"I wish I'd brought my Dramamine!"

Roy shook his head. "Calm as it is, you won't need it today."

Lester throttled back, shifted gears and eased the boat out into the channel. "It's a Gray Marine," Roy said. "First V-8 on the creek."

"Is that a fact?" Rud said.

Roy lay on top of the small forward cabin and watched the sunrise. The bay was as smooth as thermometer mercury, motionless except for the groundswell that moved through the water like a large animal under a blanket. The slow rolling motion almost rocked Roy to sleep, but his father sat rigidly upright, his hands fastened to the rim of the deck like claws. With every swell he pushed up as if riding a horse. Roy reached over and touched his father's arm. "Just relax," he said. "Don't fight it."

"Right," Rud said.

Roy wished his father hadn't come. These things never worked. Once he'd tried to show his father how to read and break peelers, and his father somehow managed to get both his thumbs crushed. Roy still wasn't sure exactly how it happened. One minute his father had the crab safely by the back fins; the next minute the crab had him by the thumbs. His father howled in pain, and Roy — like a fool, he knew, but it was before he realized how much it hurt — laughed. He hadn't meant to, but it all happened so fast it was like magic, like sleight of hand. Another time he tried to show his father how to shuck an oyster and the oyster ended up in small pieces and the oyster knife, stuck into the palm of his father's hand. At least that time Roy didn't laugh.

Lester and Otha tied the big boat to the pound net stakes, climbed over into the skiff they'd towed out, and paddled around to the top of the net. Lester leaned over and pulled up a line and lashed it to a stake. "That's the anchor line to the pound net," Roy said. "And that one holds the funnel between the false pound and the pound open."

His father nodded and swallowed.

Lester shoved the top line of a loose section of net underwater with the oar and in the same motion slid the skiff over the net. "Did you see that?" Roy said, but his father was looking the other way.

Lester and Otha paddled to the far side of the pound and worked a slack piece of net up so that all the fish were between them and the big boat, but still deep and out of sight. As they pulled themselves towards the Mary V., Roy moved to the edge of the deck. "This is the good part," he said. "This is where it gets exciting."

"I think I'll go sit up there for a while," his father said, pointing to the very bow.

"What?"

"I think I'll feel better if I can see the land."

"But you'll miss the best part."

"I'm sorry. It can't be helped." His father went and sat on the bow and stared inland at the beach and the trees and the fields. Roy watched him for a moment, then turned away and watched the fishing.

As Lester and Otha tightened the net, the trapped fish became increasingly frantic. Small fish drove their noses through the mesh. Larger fish shimmied up the sides of the net. Fish leapt into the air. They churned the water to a froth.

"A few spot," Lester said, as he and Otha slacked the net to settle the fish.

"How many boxes you think you got?" Roy said.

"Hard to tell," Lester said. "We got a few though."

Roy shook his head. He'd bet anything Lester had those fish sorted, weighed and sold already and knew the price to the nearest dollar.

Lester looked up from the fish for a moment, removed his cap and wiped his forehead with his arm. "Is your father all right?"

"Yeah, he's fine," Roy said. "He just wanted to see the farm from another angle. You know how these real estate people are." Roy was glad when Lester started bailing fish, because Roy did not want to talk about his father. The less said about his father the better. Roy did not want to be the son of someone who got sea sick.

While Otha bailed the undersized fish and sea nettles overboard, Lester bailed the good fish into the Mary V. The first netfuls of fish made a hollow drumming sound against the floorboards. Then, as fish piled on fish, there was a flat drumming sound, and a fine mist of fish slime and seawater rose a foot or so above the fish. Then the drumming quieted and the mist disappeared, as the fish settled, their gills flared, colors darkened, and their markings became more distinct: the deep gold of the spot; the dark green along the backs of the bluefish that turned silver along the belly; the mottled brown and silver of the grey trout and croaker; the sharp black spots of the speckled trout; the mother-of-pearl sides of the butterfish. But they weren't all beautiful. The oyster toad's head looked like it had been stepped on; its lower jaw jutted out like a drawer full of teeth. Its brown slimy skin bristled with spines. The swell toads were more foolish looking than ugly, with their headlight eyes and rabbit teeth and habit of inflating themselves with air so that in the boat they'd lie around like volleyballs. If space became a problem, a pocket knife was the solution.

When Lester finished bailing fish, he climbed back into the big boat and rolled a barrel on its edge over to the gunnel. When he stood the barrel upright, fish squirted out from under it like spit watermelon seeds. He started sorting the crabs that Otha handed up one netful at a time. "Are you sure your father's all right?"

"Oh, yeah, he's fine," Roy said.

"I think if it was my father, I might want to go and check on him."

Roy did not want to check on his father, but since Lester had asked, what could he do? Lester was the captain of that boat, and the captain had absolute authority. So Roy said, "All right," and slowly, reluctantly, moved up and sat beside his father.

"So how you doing?" Roy asked.

His father shrugged noncommittally. His skin was the color of seawater.

"No better, huh?"

His father shook his head and swallowed.

"You're not going to get sick, are you?"

His father swallowed again.

"Damn — I mean darn. I hope you don't get sick. You think you can hold it 'til we get back?"

His father sighed.

"The other nets are hung up drying," Roy said. "This is the only net we're going to fish today. Thirty, forty minutes at the most and we'll be back on shore."

"Thank God," his father said through a narrow slit.

"That bad, huh? I'll tell you what, we'll make a deal. If you don't get sick, when we get back, we'll go play golf. I mean it. As soon as we get back, we'll go over to the bayshore. O.K.?"

His father looked at him, his eyes, glazed and weary. "Please leave me alone," he said. Then his mouth clamped shut like an oyster.

"O.K., O.K., I'm leaving. I wouldn't have bothered you in the first place except Lester made me." He patted his father on the leg. "I hope you feel better."

Roy scooted back to where he'd been sitting. Lester shook a large jimmy crab off the end of his heavy rubber glove into a bushel basket, then dumped the sooks and smaller males, all connected by their claws, into the barrel. "So how's your father doing?" Lester asked.

"Well," Roy said. "I guess he is a little under the weather. We've all had a touch of the flu. He had it worse'n any of us. I thought he was over it, but I guess not. He'll be all right, though. He'll shake it off. I'm telling you, these Simons are tough. They're almost as tough as Harmons."

Then his father leaned out over the bow as far as he could and vomited profusely for several minutes.

"Damn flu bug," Roy said. "I knew he shouldn't have come. And he shouldn't have drank all that beer last night either, tired as he was from driving. I've never seen a man could drink so much beer."

His father sat up, wiped his face with his handkerchief, blew his nose, and took a few deep breaths. "I do not have the flu," he announced in a raspy voice. "And I am not hung over. I am sea sick. Is that such a crime?"

"Jesus Christ!" Roy thought.

"Well, is it?"

"No, indeed," Lester said. "If it was, there'd be some watermen right here on this creek that would be in jail. Isn't that right, Otha?"

"Yes, my Lord," Otha said. "Cap'n Jimmy, he'd be doing life."

"Jimmy Gaskins?" Roy said.

"He gets sick every time he goes out," Lester said. "Least that's what they tell me."

"I never heard that before," Roy said.

"It's the truth," Otha said. "He goes down below, does what he has to do, then comes back up and goes right on about his business."

"Otha knows, too," Lester said. "He used to work for him."

"That I did. Worked seven winters drudging oysters all the way up to the Potomac River."

"Otha's not real loyal," Lester said. "He'll work for anybody that pays him enough."

"And some that don't," Otha said.

Rud moved down and sat beside his son. "Usually I take Dramamine," he said, "But I left in such a hurry this morning, I forgot it. If I don't take it, just like clockwork. Something about those swells."

"That's just the way it was with Cap'n Jimmy," Otha said. "He didn't mind a rough sea much as he did a ground swell. Just exactly the same. He might even be a kin of yours."

"No, all my people are from inland."

"I'd of never known that," Otha said. "I'd of taken you for a Guineaman myself. Wouldn't you, Cap'n Les?"

"Either that or a Tangierman," Lester said.

"No, my Lawd," Otha said. "Got too much sense to be a Tangierman. And he talks too plain."

"I guess if I had much sense, I'd have stayed on shore."

"You can't keep a Guineaman on shore," Otha said. "Any waterman, he got to be on the water."

"I'm no waterman," Rud said.

"Got to be a little bit," Otha said. "Any man come out knowing he going to get sick, he's got to love the water. Ain't that right?"

"Darn right," Lester said. "He's got to love it more'n I do, I'll tell you that. I couldn't do it. I'd have to get me an office job in the city, with a big desk and a nice young secretary to take care of me."

"Now you talking," Otha said handing up a netful of crabs. "Now you saying something. It would be goodbye, Mr. Sea Nettle, you done stung me the last time."

Lester laughed. "What'd the preacher say, Otha?"

"Preacher? He say, 'My, my, those are nice tomatoes.'"

They both laughed at the private joke.

"And what did Wheeler say?"

"He say, 'Slow'er down, Cheetum. Slow'er down.'"

They both laughed again, and this time Roy's father laughed with them, as if he too understood the joke, but Roy, who knew all about the wino, Wheeler, and the preacher who mooched tomatoes (and fish and crabs — whatever was in season) did not laugh. He sat quietly and stared off at the different colored crab pot buoys that dotted the bay like decorations, and at the crab potters, moving slowly along the strings of pots. There was C.E. Lee in the Jean, and Junior Boy Willis, who used his wife to pull his pots by hand long after the others had gone to mechanical winders. And there was Jeter Jenkins, who couldn't talk plain, and Crittenden Campbell in the Three Kids, only now there were just two, because one had suffocated trying to keep warm in the small cabin one cold day when his father was oystering back of the marshes.

Roy could recognize them all even from half a mile away: the Jean by the way her bow rose straight up out of the water — she had the most deadrise on the creek — and Junior Boy Willis' wife by the way she stayed hunched over even when she wasn't pulling pots, and Jeter Jenkins by his big belly, and Crittenden Campbell by the way he rocked back and forth at the tiller. Roy knew them all, and they knew him, and they would talk to him when they pulled alongside the Mary V. for bait, the boats sometimes three deep, and the men, even in rough weather, walking gunnel to engine box to gunnel as easily as other men might walk down the street. They wouldn't talk to him like he was a "come-hither" either. They talked to him like he belonged, like he was one of them, because they knew that Roy knew the fish and the boats and the water. He knew the bay. And now his father, who didn't know anything, didn't know how to dress or how to talk or how to act, was being treated like a big hero — by Otha and Lester, of all people! For what? For puking overboard, as if that was some great accomplishment, like knowing how to read a peeler or shuck an oyster or recognize a boat from half a mile away.

"You feel all right?" his father said. "You're awfully quiet."

"Yeah, I feel fine," Roy said.

"You sure? You've been so quiet."

"Don't worry about it, O.K.?"

"I hope you're not getting it too. Maybe it runs in the family."

"No," Roy said. "It does not run in the family. Not in the Harmon family, anyway."

His father stared at him. They were both quiet now. Now everybody was quiet except Otha, who had started humming this gospel, spiritual type hymn that Roy hated. That was one thing about Otha; when the going got rough, he would sometimes slip into this Uncle Remus character. Lester could disappoint you too, but at least he didn't hum.

"Well, I hope you feel all right," his father finally said. Then, turning away, "I certainly feel a lot better."

"You look like you do," Lester said. "Your color's a whole lot better."

"That's just how it was with Cap'n Jimmy," Otha said. "He got sick, but he didn't stay sick."

Roy wished Otha would shut up about Jimmy Gaskins. Roy knew Jimmy Gaskins. Many a day he'd sat with binoculars and watched Jimmy Gaskins bring his boat back into the creek. Jimmy would stand there with his head cocked back and little cap tipped low over his eyes to shield them from the setting sun, one hand tucked behind his oilskin apron, the other on the wheel. He'd dock that big boat — it was close to seventy feet — with two swishes of its tail. It had twin screws; he could turn it on a dime. When he hit the throttle that last time, just before he killed the engine, you could hear the rumble all the way across the creek.

Roy rode back lying on the bow. The sun bore down on him, and salt spray flew into his face. A flock of gulls dove in the wake for scraps of fish, and a pair of ospreys peered over the edge of their nest on the black beacon. By the time they got back to the dock, Roy felt better. The bay always did that. It was like a medicine. For some people.

Roy walked his father back to the car. He said he was sorry he talked like he did. He didn't know what got into him sometimes. His father said not to worry about it; it didn't matter. At least now he knew where he belonged.

"You did all right," Roy said. "They thought so."

"Well, that's what counts, isn't it?" Rud said. Then he smiled.

Roy couldn't tell if his father was serious or not. That happened a lot.

"Well, I'm going to hit some golf balls," his father said. "You can come if you like, but don't feel obligated."

"I guess I'll hang around and help Lester and Otha sort fish," Roy said.

"O.K."

Roy watched his father walk across the lawn to his car. He seemed surprisingly spry. Roy waited until the car disappeared up the lane. Then he walked back down to the dock. He put on a pair of short rubber boots and rubber gloves and slid down into the Mary V. Otha and Lester were tossing fish into boxes and baskets. Their hands moved so fast fish were always in the air. Roy scooped up three spot and tossed them into a bushel basket.

"Your father seems to be feeling better," Lester said.

"I guess he is," Roy said. "He's gone off to hit some golf balls."

Lester stood up and stretched his back. "Now there's a game I never could quite understand. Must be something to it, though, as many people as play it. But darned if I could figure if out. Could you, Otha?"

"No, my Lord. I wouldn't know one end of a golf ball from the other."

"Me either," Lester said.

"That makes three of us," Roy said.

Roy liked wading around in the fish. He liked the weight of the fish on his boots and the feel of them in his hands. He even liked how they smelled. Only city people thought fish stunk. He liked everything about the place, but what he liked best was working alongside Lester and Otha, listening to their banter. They were good people, the best, and if they sometimes went a little too far in trying to make an outsider feel at home, well, you couldn't hold that against them. That's just how they were.

"That was nice what you did for my father," Roy said.

"What's that?" Lester said, tossing a big grey trout into a basket.

"That business about Jimmy Gaskins."

"We didn't do anything for you father."

"That man does for himself," Otha said.

Well, naturally they weren't going to admit it to him, but Roy knew for a fact — he'd bet anything — that Jimmy Gaskins had never been seasick a day in his life.

Mates For Life

Lester didn't know exactly what the problem was, but all the pleasure seemed to be going out of life. One thing that usually cheered him up was hunting, but doves were all that was in season, and Harmons didn't hunt doves.

They hunted geese, though, and there were a lot of geese around. The only problem was, the season didn't open for another six weeks. So, either Lester would have to not hunt, violate a family tradition by shooting doves, or break the law. Once he saw the problem in those terms, he knew exactly what to do. He would call his lifelong friend, C.E. Lee for a legal opinion, not as to whether Lester's plan was legal or not — he knew that — but to find out if it was illegal enough to even interest a man of C.E. Lee's credentials.

A few years back, C.E. Lee had run a commercial hunting operation over bait. He built a set of stake blinds, to and from which he ferried city people in his workboat. If any of his clients asked why, with so much water to chose from, the ducks simply flew from one of C.E.'s stake blinds to the other, C.E. would tip his little green cap back, scratch his head, get a far off look in his eye, and explain how in the course of a lifetime, a man developed a special feeling for the wind and tides, the flight patterns and feeding habits of waterfowl. He never once mentioned bait. The game wardens, being less gullible than C.E.'s clients, closed him down in the first year.

The phone rang for several minutes before C.E. Lee picked it up. His voice, could it somehow have been recorded and attached to a pack of cigarettes, could have replaced the Surgeon's General's warning.

Lester said a flock of geese was practically taking over his lower field. They were ruining his winter wheat. Wouldn't a man be within his rights if he took a shot at one? Even in this day and age, didn't a man have a right to defend his property?

"What time is it?" C.E. growled.

"Two o'clock," Lester said. "A little after. Did I wake you up?"

"Not yet," C.E. said, slamming down the receiver.

Lester took a cold six pack of beer and sat outside on the brick stoop in the mild mid-October afternoon air and waited for his friend. He knew C.E. would come no matter how hungover he was. C.E. would never admit it, but he was very loyal, to his friends and to his alcohol, but in that order. There was something indomitable about the man that even Lester had to admire.

For example, most men, caught red-handed baiting ducks, would have pleaded guilty and thrown themselves upon the mercy of the court, but not C.E. Lee. He fought every inch of the way, and such was his hatred of lawyers, he represented himself in court. He argued that in the long run baiting was good for ducks. He said it was a conservation measure. Sure, a few ducks got killed, but the rest were better nourished, stronger, healthier, and more likely to survive their migration and reproduce, to create more ducks. And really, when you got right down to it, wasn't that what they were all working towards? The judge threw the book at him.

Lester heard C.E.'s truck banging down the rutted dirt lane before he saw it. Then a roostertail of dust rose above the hedgerow that bordered the lane, and C.E. Lee rounded the bend. He drove the last stretch as if he were trying to plane his truck across the tops of the corrugations the way you'd run a skiff in a light chop. He skidded to a halt in the edge of Lester's yard and fought his way through the cloud of dust he'd created. "When are you going to put a load of gravel on that road?" C.E. said, dust still swirling about his head, "It's rough as a cob."

"You try driving around some of those holes," Lester said, "you might not find the going quite so rough."

"I guess that's what they make shock absorbers for isn't it?"

"Your truck might last a little longer if you figured out what they made the steering wheel for."

"Don't worry about my truck. Is one of those for me?"

Lester handed him a beer. C.E. ripped the top off and slapped the foaming can to his mouth. C.E. was a larger man than Lester and losing his hair, which explained the little green hat. It was like part of his head. Looked more natural to Lester than some hair pieces he'd seen. C.E.'s skin hadn't handled the weather as well as Lester's. His face was puffier and pinker. Part of that might have been the alcohol.

C.E. lowered the now half empty can. "So where're all the geese?" he said, wiping his mouth.

"Well," Lester said, "right now I'd say they're up at the head of Cobb's Creek. A fellow up that way has got a permit to feed them. So they sit out there all day, and come down here towards evening and feed all night in my lower field."

"A permit?"

"Nowadays you got to have a federal permit to feed geese."

"Why don't we have one?"

Sometimes C.E. Lee struck Lester as being world wise and sophisticated. Other times he seemed just plain stupid. "The permit," Lester said, "doesn't allow you to shoot them, just feed them."

"Why in the world would anyone want to do that?"

"I don't know," Lester said. "Some people just do."

They rode in C.E.'s truck to the bridge, and from there walked to the end of the lower field. Lester paused now and then to point out goose droppings to his companion. C.E. was not impressed. He picked up a specimen, crumbled it in his fist, tossed the fine powder into the wind. "It's old," he said.

30

They concealed themselves in the brush at the end of the lower field, their backs towards the beach. No blind was necessary. The sky over the field, except for an occasional dove, was empty. "If the game warden comes, we can say we were shooting doves," Lester said.

C.E. scowled and shook his head. "I'd sooner go to jail than admit to shooting one of those little things. Like shooting songbirds."

C.E. Lee had very strict ethical standards, though they did not necessarily coincide with the law. In fact, they usually didn't. Lester admired how his friend stuck to his principles, whatever the consequences. He lived as he drove, rarely altering his course for obstacles. He did spend an inordinate amount of time in jail, though. Nothing serious — game laws, traffic violations, delinquent alimony — that was about it. It was the jail time, Lester thought, that explained the longevity of C.E.'s truck, plus the time he was without a license. Not that that stopped him from driving, but it made him drive more cautiously so as not to attract attention. Though, of course, it had the exact opposite effect: nothing was more conspicuous than the sight of C.E. Lee's truck being driven cautiously.

"When do you suppose," Lester said after a long silence, "was the last time we hunted legally?"

"I don't know," C.E. said. "I don't want to think about it either. Makes me feel too old."

"And yet we hunt the same as we always hunted, pretty much the same way our fathers hunted."

"So?"

"So when was it that we became criminals?"

C.E. thought for a moment. "When they changed the laws, I guess, and we didn't change our ways."

"I don't feel like a criminal," Lester said. "Do you?"

"No, indeed. The way I see it, we're out here doing a civic duty. They don't make these laws to protect wildlife, you know. They do it to raise revenues, by tripping up and fining people such as ourselves, who can't keep up with all the changes. You practically have to be a lawyer to understand the rule book."

"Never looked at it like that," Lester said.

"Well, you ought to. You ought to take pride in how you live your life. You can't go skulking around. Without the likes of you and me, they wouldn't need wardens. We're creating jobs by being out here, and the money we pay in fines — though I can't say you've paid your share — goes for schools and highways and who knows what all. Of course, they've got to catch us first."

It was almost sunset before the first small flock of geese appeared in the northern sky.

"Here they come." Lester said. "Right on schedule."

"I see them."

The two men hunkered in the tall grass, guns ready.

But the geese did not begin their descent until they were beyond the field and over the pine woods at the head of Muddy Creek.

"They're going down in the creek," Lester said. "I've never seen 'em do that before."

"I knew we should have put out decoys," C.E. said.

"And advertise the fact that we're hunting out of season?"

C.E. snarled, "If I'm gonna be caught for hunting out of season, I want to be caught hunting successfully out of season, you understand? I got a reputation in this county. That means something to me, though I wouldn't expect you to understand."

Lester was glad of that, because he most certainly didn't understand. Lester's idea of the perfect crime, to the extent that he even thought about it, was one where you didn't get caught. C.E. seemed to have a different idea. With C.E. it was the quality of the crime that counted. Even if Lester didn't understand it, he still sort of admired it. "Maybe the next bunch will come in here," Lester said. "They've been coming in here right regular."

But the next flock followed the exact same flight pattern as the first, and soon there was a steady flow of geese high over the field heading towards Muddy Creek. It was beautiful to watch, the patterns carefully arranged to break the wind, and the formations constantly shifting so no goose had to take the lead for long, or so Lester had been told. Geese were majestic, intelligent birds, and they mated for life, which made Lester respect them all the more, but not want to hunt them any less. Only a non-hunter would see that as a contradiction.

Lester looked at his watch and at the fading light in the west. "Soon be too dark to shoot."

"It's never too dark to shoot," C.E. said.

At first Lester took that as just another of C.E.'s inscrutable remarks. Gradually, though, as he stood watching the geese stream across the sky, it sunk in what his partner said, and he was filled with the sense of being in the presence of a higher intelligence, or if not higher, certainly a very different one. "You know," Lester said, "you might have just put your finger on something."

"My grandfather used to talk a lot about punt gunning," C.E. said.

"Mine too," Lester said. "Wish I'd paid more attention."

"Not that much to it," C.E. said, as if he'd been doing it all his life, instead of just dreaming of it. "Wouldn't take five minutes to pull a headlight out of my truck. Fasten it to the bow of your boat, hook it to a twelve volt battery, we'd be in business."

"Have to wrap the oarlocks in burlap," Lester said, "to keep them quiet."

"One row, one shoot."

"Might work."

"I don't see why it wouldn't."

"You know," Lester said, "just thinking of that fellow feeding those geese makes me want to shoot one all the more. Now isn't that a terrible way to be?"

"Would make more sense to shoot him."

"In some ways it would."

"Ought to let us feed the geese," C.E. said. "We feed them. They feed us. The cycle of nature, the way the good Lord intended it to be. I'll always believe that."

They practically ran back to the truck, and this time C.E.'s normal driving speed was none too fast for Lester. At the bridge they noted the tide was running strongly through the ditch into Muddy Creek. Soon it would turn and run the other way; there was no time to waste.

For all the quarreling the two men did, they worked extremely well together when they had a project they both believed in. The headlight was removed from C.E.'s truck with surgical efficiency, the right tool appearing at his fingertips at precisely the right time. But in the age of plastic feed bags, burlap was harder to come by. The only piece they could locate held Lester's duck decoys. He hated to ruin that, but it was for a good cause, and it was quickly split and the oarlocks swaddled until each oar could be moved though a silent arc.

It was dark when they departed Lester's dock. They ran the engine slowly to the head of Muddy creek and rowed from there. C.E. rowed, and Lester sat in the bow beside the light and his gun, because Lester was the better shot. Even C.E. Lee acknowledged that.

There was no moon, but once Lester's eyes had adapted to the dark, he could make out the silhouettes of the scraggly pine, pin oak and wild persimmon along the beach, and to his right an open space he knew to be the field behind the Simons'.

Soon a black wall replaced the opening. That meant they were past the field and had reached the tall stand of red pine — first land you raised coming across the bay — that bordered the narrow waist of Muddy Creek. It also meant they weren't far from where the geese went down. C.E. stopped rowing, and both men listened intently. Ahead they could hear the feeding sounds of hundreds, maybe a thousand, geese. It was a low cackling sound, with only an occasional higher pitched squawk. It made Lester's heart beat fast, and he touched his gun, light, and battery, just to get his bearings.

"Plenty of time yet," C.E. whispered.

"I know," Lester whispered back.

Lester peered into the darkness, but he could see nothing. C.E. rowed slowly towards the sounds, which grew more diffuse as the skiff approached. Soon the sounds were on both sides of them, then behind them as well. They were surrounded by geese; they had rowed into the middle of the flock, which was scattered widely across the creek. C.E. leaned back towards Lester. "I think we're here," he whispered.

Lester's hand trembled as he tried to connect the cable to the battery terminal. When he finally made contact the glare of the light, after such intense darkness, blinded him, and the noise, the shrieks of a thousand, or maybe fifteen hundred — the numbers would grow over the years — startled geese, and the roar of the wings hammering the water as they frantically fought for altitude, unnerved both men. They fired late, and did not hit a single goose. They looked hopefully for a while, feeling that with so many geese in the air they must have hit something. The water was covered with feathers, but evenly covered. There were no clumps to indicate a hit. These were feathers shed in the course of feeding, preening, and panicky flight.

Lester slumped back in the bow of the boat and lit a cigarette. C.E. kept rowing and searching. "A cripple might have tried to make it across the beach," he said.

"Might have," Lester said. Lester hoped they'd find at least one goose. They'd gone to so much trouble. He felt like he'd let them down. Even though both men had shot, Lester was the one they'd counted on to hit a goose. C.E. had done his part. He put them in the center of the flock. What more could you ask of the oarman?

The tide had fallen and left a margin of smooth sand along the water's edge, perfect for recording footprints. But the beach was unblemished. "Clean as a baby's bottom," C.E. said.

"Looks like we would have hit at least one," Lester said. "Hard to see how you could miss, as many geese as were in the air." He knew that was a lie. The first lesson of quail hunting was, no matter how large the covey, or how close, you selected one bird, and only after that bird fell did you move to another target. He knew that as well as he knew anything; he just hadn't ever had to apply it to geese.

"If we could have just got a shot off while they were on the water," C.E. said.

"Couldn't see," Lester said. "And when I turned that light on, I really couldn't see."

"Near about blinded me too," C.E. said. "Must've been on high beam."

"Must've been."

There was nothing to do but turn around and row home. The creek was too shallow now to run the engine.

"You want me to row?" Lester said.

"Naw, I'll do it."

"I feel like I ought to do something."

"You've done plenty."

"I guess I have."

"Don't take it so hard. Hell, everything worked perfect except one part."

"Pretty big part, though."

"Aw, Les, come on. There's a lot more to hunting than killing, even illegal hunting. You know that."

"I guess so," Lester said.

"How many men can honestly say they snuck into the middle of a flock of feeding geese? Darn few I'd say. I bet there's not two other men in this county that have done it, or could have. You got to have the know-how, the technical expertise, to pull off a deal like this. Those old timers, they weren't punting geese. They were punting redheads and canvasbacks, dumb ducks. But to get right in the middle of a flock wild geese — hell, you ought to feel proud."

"Put it like that, maybe I should," Lester said, and the fact was, he did a little bit. He certainly didn't feel ashamed any more. He didn't really understand it. C.E. just had a way of looking at things, and a way of explaining them, that wasn't exactly how Lester would have explained them, but you couldn't say C.E. hadn't told the truth. In some ways it was better than the truth; it was the truth, the whole truth, and then some.

"I'll tell you another thing, partner," C.E. said. "We might not have hit a single goose, but we certainly put the fear of God in all of them."

"We did that," Lester said.

"Enough goose shit dropped in thirty seconds to fertilize your whole lower field."

"All of that," Lester said, "and maybe the creek field too."

They both laughed, and C.E. stopped rowing and lit another cigarette. It was a mild night, cool, but not cold, and there was no great hurry to get home. So they let the skiff drift with the falling tide, while they smoked and chatted and made plans for next year.

Next year they were going to camouflage one of Lester's boats; they'd make a floating blind and anchor it just upwind of where that fellow was feeding geese. Probably wouldn't even need decoys. It would

be pass shooting at its finest, just like the old days.
No, better.

Pilgrims

Contrary to what some people thought, Sharon Harmon did not want to change Lester or take over his life, but she did have to admit he was a challenge to her vision of one big happy family.

Sharon had had a lonely childhood, the only daughter of a professionally obsessed father and a mother who was adept at everything except motherhood. Star had wooed Sharon with stories of growing up on a farm surrounded by siblings and cousins and with tales of huge holiday dinners. She was infatuated, and soon they married and promptly, much to her dismay, moved to California. It was a career move for Star, who was a purchasing agent for a large department store. Sharon, an elementary school teacher, could teach anywhere. They told themselves the move was temporary; California was full of transients. Soon they'd be moving on like all the others.

But the years passed, and promotion followed promotion — Star was good at what he did — and Sharon built up seniority in the school system and was invested in the state retirement. It seemed a shame to give all that up. So they postponed moving back East until they both retired. But by then all the older generation had died off, and none of the younger ones had moved back yet. Of the three old home places, Lester lived alone in one; the Simons used another for vacations, and the third was hammered shut. Sam and Elsie Harmon were supposed to have built their place. Three times they'd cleared their point, but somehow never got around to building. "We've got such close ties in Baltimore," they said.

"We have ties in California," Sharon said. "We're moving anyway." Which was exactly what they did. "Somebody has to be first," Sharon said. "I'm not afraid."

Now in November of her first year back, with winter fast approaching, she was afraid. She was afraid that her retirement years would be as lonely as her childhood. "If only we'd had children," she thought. They'd tried. She wished now they'd tried harder, sought medical help, but Star said no. "If we were meant to have children," he said, "then we'll have children." Later she would begrudge him that fatalistic attitude — at menopause she was furious — but gradually she learned to accept what she couldn't change, and the resentment subsided. Only now the loneliness was back.

The farm seemed bleaker, more barren, than she'd remembered it: the bare fields, the leafless trees, the brown grass, and the endless grey reaches of the Chesapeake, which she'd remembered as bluish green. The loneliness was so familiar; it made her cry. Then she caught herself and said, "No." A child had no control over its environment, but she was not a child any more. True, she couldn't change the fact that the Simons had chosen this of all Thanksgivings to go to Florida, or that Sam and Elsie were apt to procrastinate forever, but that did not mean she and Star and Lester couldn't have a perfectly satisfactory Thanksgiving. They would make the most of what they had, each other. Wasn't that the real spirit of Thanksgiving?

"You can invite him, if you want to," Star said, when he heard her plan, "but I doubt he'll come."

"Of course, he'll come. Why on earth wouldn't he come?"

"The men on that side of the family always go bird hunting on Thanksgiving day. Thanksgiving and Christmas."

"He can go bird hunting any day of the week."

"Can and often does, but Thanksgiving is different. He feels he pretty much has to go then. Sort of like going to church, I guess."

"Well, I'm not asking him to give up the whole day, just to share Thanksgiving dinner with us. Is that such a sacrifice?"

"He might come."

"Well, call him and see. No, I'll call him."

Lester tried a variety of excuses. He was going bird

hunting (she was ready for that); he and C.E. Lee might be doing something together (bring him too; the more the merrier); he had been trying to lose weight and didn't think he could eat a big meal (eat as little as he liked; just eat it with them; that's all she was asking). Finally he said awright, maybe he would come.

"Maybe?"

"You can pretty much count on it," Lester said. "Might not stay real long, though."

"Stay however long you like. We'll see you then."

She hung up the phone and gave her husband a triumphant nod. "There, you see, nothing to it."

"He's not here yet," Star said.

On Thanksgiving morning Sharon was up at first light, chopping and dicing, stuffing and trussing. Star helped. He was very handy in the kitchen. It was his best room, not that she cared about the other any more except as it related to family. But this day she was feeling rich with family.

"Let's do this every year," she said. "Next year, Rud and Miriam. Then — who knows? — maybe Sam and Elsie and some of the others." Many of the relatives were planning on moving back.

"Let's get through this year first," Star said.

"Oh, this is nothing. This will be a piece of cake."

She'd made plenty of Thanksgiving dinners before, but this one was special. In California none of the people she entertained cared that much about Thanksgiving. It was considered an eastern tradition, which was what they had come west to escape. "This is better than California, isn't it?" Sharon said.

"I told you it would be," Star said.

Lester showed up one hour late wearing hunting clothes and muddy boots. He brought his bird dog, Sarge, which he tied to a freshly planted azalea bush. The bush's root system was no match for the dog's strength. Sarge dragged the bush around the yard like a sea anchor.

"Don't guess I should have tied him to that," Lester said, "but I didn't see what else to tie him to?" They had cleared the point of all vegetation except around the shoreline.

"No harm done, " Star said, after he'd recovered and replanted his prize bush. "They're dormant this time of year anyway."

They secured Sarge to the bumper of Star's Buick station wagon and went inside. Lester wiped his boots off as best he could and left his gun outside on the porch. "I would have been here sooner," Lester said, "but darned if Sarge didn't start a covey of birds on the way over."

"Is that a fact?" Star said.

"I wasn't even really hunting," Lester said. "Just walking."

"Did you get a shot?"

"No, indeed. My gun wasn't even loaded. The darn things got up wild and flew across the head of the cove to the old orchard point. The dog went after them."

"Sam and Elsie's place," Star said to Sharon, who didn't know the family names for the different parts of the farm.

"I had to wade across the marsh to get my dog back."

"You could have walked around on the road."

"I guess I could have, but that would have taken

44

time, and I didn't want to be too late."

"That's was thoughtful of you," Star said. "Wasn't it?" he added turning to his wife.

"Yes, it was," Sharon said.

"Did you find any single birds?" Star said.

"Didn't look for them," Lester said. "But I have a pretty good idea where they went. I promised Sarge I'd take him back after dinner and try to find them. Just about broke his heart to pull him away. Probably why he was so riled up when he got here."

"I imagine it was," Star said.

"You two make yourselves comfortable in the living room," Sharon said. "I think there's a football game on. I've got a few more things to do in the kitchen."

Sharon walked very deliberately back into the kitchen. She completed her dinner preparations at her normal rate of speed, neither faster nor slower than usual. She would never intentionally interfere with Lester's hunting plans, but neither would she be rushed by promises he had made to a dog.

The peas were ruined, and the rolls were hard as lumps of clay. So, she would make more rolls and peas. The rest, the turkey, dressing, potatoes, gravy, cranberry sauce, congealed salad, could be salvaged. Most importantly, the pièce de résistance, the sweet potato pie, Lester's favorite, was still perfect. Room temperature, that was how Star said it should be served.

Soon Star came into the kitchen to see how dinner was progressing. "Everything is coming along very nicely," Sharon said.

"Could you give me an idea about how much longer it will be. Lester's getting a little restless."

"Not much longer," Sharon said.

"What do you suppose I ought to tell him? Ten? Fifteen minutes?"

"Tell him it will be ready when it's ready."

"I'll tell him fifteen minutes."

"Whatever you think is best."

When Sharon began putting food on the table, Lester was already seated. He had his napkin tucked into his shirt; there was an expectant, eager look on his face. He reminded Sharon of one of her third graders.

Star took his seat at one end of the large dining room table, which they almost never used. Sharon sat at the other. Lester reached for the plate of steaming rolls. Sharon admonished him with a tone of voice she hadn't used for years, "Not until we've said grace." And the gesture, the index finger lifted, held aloft, not aimed — that was too threatening for third graders. Then to her husband, "Darling, would you care to say grace."

"You go ahead," Star said.

They shut their eyes and bowed their heads; Sharon last. "Our Father, we thank You for this day and for our many blessings," she began, speaking slowly, each word carefully chosen. No standard blessing on this special day; this would be original. "We thank You for the bounty of the land and of the sea, and most of all we thank You for this family. We ask that You bless each and every member of this family, those who were not able to be here this day, and those who were." There was the sound of someone pouring water. Sharon opened one eye, and Lester sheepishly put the pitcher down and shut his eyes. "In Jesus name, Amen," Sharon said.

"Amen," Lester and Star said in unison with what Sharon thought was unnecessary emphasis.

The dining room table, which Sharon had bought with huge family meals in mind, was so large that Star and Sharon could not reach each other with the food. Every dish that was passed had to go through Lester's hands. This could have seriously interfered with his eating if he had let it, but he didn't. He ate with one hand and passed food with the other. If two dishes to be passed arrived at the same time, one simply had to wait. Sometimes, such as when he needed two hands to cut turkey, both dishes had to wait.

Sharon took her time serving and eating, and when she spoke, she made it sound as if they had all afternoon to sit and linger at the table, just the way Star said it used to be. "So, Lester," she said, wiping her mouth, "Star tells me that you go quail hunting every Thanksgiving, that it's sort of a tradition on your side of the family."

Lester nodded and continued chewing his food. When he swallowed that mouthful, instead of saying anything, he took another bite from the fork he'd been refilling with turkey, dressing, peas and mashed potatoes while chewing his food.

"I like traditions," Sharon said, poking a few peas with the tines of her fork. "I think they're very important, don't you?"

"Um humh," Lester said.

These yes and no questions were getting her nowhere; so Sharon changed her tactics. "Tell me, Lester, what is it about quail hunting that is so intriguing? What makes quail hunting so special? Star tells me it's different from other types of hunting."

Lester swallowed and wiped his mouth. "Hard to explain," he said, taking another bite, though "bite" hardly described the amount of food that was entering his mouth with each fork load. His fork overflowed with food. (The slab of turkey on the end was the key; it kept the other food from falling off, and, of course, the peas had to go on right after the mashed potatoes; otherwise they'd roll off).

"Well, try to explain, would you? I really am interested." Lester got a thoughtful, troubled look on his face, and Sharon knew she had him. She'd asked him about a subject he was actually interested in. Oldest trick in the book for reticent children.

"It's the birds," Lester said between bites. "The birds and the dog."

"What about the birds and the dog?"

"Have to ask them," Lester said, his mouth half full.

Star chuckled. Sharon quieted him with a quick sharp look, then turned back to Lester, and waited. It took patience to be a good teacher, but often the most difficult students were the most rewarding. Anyone could teach the well motivated child.

Lester wiped his mouth. He rubbed his chin and looked out the window. Then he turned back to Sharon. "The smell of the birds excites the dog," he said slowly. "The dog's excitement excites the hunter. The key is the dog. He has to be there. The same way you need me sitting between you and Star. Without me here to pass food, you'd starve to death." They laughed. "Well, the dog passes information to the hunter. The way he moves, the look in his eyes, how his tail wags. You can find birds without a dog. I've

48

walked up many a covey and it's a surprise, it's a shock, they make a racket, but it's not exciting. Got to have the dog." Lester nodded, meaning that was all he had to say about that.

"Thank you, Lester," Sharon said. "That was most informative." Then she gave a little nod to her husband, indicating that not only did Lester come and eat, he talked. Total victory.

"May I be excused?" Lester said.

"Why, Lester," Sharon said, "the rest of us have barely begun eating."

"I don't mean for you to stop," Lester said.

"But you haven't had your dessert yet."

Lester patted his stomach. "I'm so full right now, I don't believe I could eat another bite."

"But Star says it's your favorite. Tell him what it is, Star."

"You tell him."

"Sweet potato pie."

Another troubled, thoughtful look crossed Lester's face. "I do like sweet potato pie," he said.

"Well, you just wait a minute or two for the rest of us to finish, and maybe your appetite will return."

Lester looked at his watch, then out the window.

"I've got an idea," Star said. "Why don't you take a slice of pie with you. I could wrap it real good in cellophane, you could put it right in your game bag. As long as you didn't lean back against it, it would keep fine."

"That's a good idea," Lester said. "I like that idea."

"Take two slices," Star said. "One for now, one for later."

"Well, if there's plenty to go around, maybe I will."

"She made it just for you, didn't you, honey?"

Sharon smiled weakly and nodded. She was left speechless by this wretched idea, this dreadful plot to ruin Thanksgiving dinner. By the time she regained her composure, the men had retreated into the kitchen, where they were cutting up the pie.

Sharon, determined not to be rude on this of all days, waited for the men at the front door. She handed Lester his hunting coat, and he gently tucked two generous slices of pie into the game bag and slipped the coat on. "Well," he said, "I certainly enjoyed my dinner. That's as good a turkey as I've ever put in my mouth."

"She makes a good turkey, doesn't she?" Star said. "Done, but not dry."

"Best I've ever had," Lester said.

"Well we're certainly glad you could come," Sharon said. "Plan to come next year, won't you? And allow yourself a little more time to eat."

"Maybe I will," Lester said. "Of course, next year is a long way off."

Meanwhile Sarge had dug two large holes in the yard and chewed though a piece of garden hose. "I don't know what's wrong with this dog. What's the matter with you anyway?" Lester said as he released the dog. Sarge dashed across the yard out into the field.

"No real harm done," Star said. "I shouldn't have left that hose there anyway."

"I'll repay you for the hose," Lester said.

"Don't even think about it."

Lester waved goodbye to Sharon, who was standing on the porch, and started up the road towards the orchard point. Sharon stood with her arms folded and watched as her husband repaired the damage to the yard. He did a very neat job, carefully separating the topsoil from the sod before filling the hole. He was quite skilled at yardwork, exceptionally skilled, she would say.

When Star approached the porch, Sharon turned away. "'I have a good idea,'" she said, in a mocking, sing-songy voice. "'Why don't you take a slice of pie with you. No take *two* slices.'" Then in a different voice, a hoarse whisper, "Like a knife in my back."

"Well, I'm sorry if you didn't think it was a good idea," Star said, "but that's just too bad. I'd had all I could take of watching him twitch and fidget, and you interrogating him like he was a prisoner. It was ruining my meal!"

Sharon, startled by her husband's little outburst, wheeled around and looked at him. They were so rare, these little explosions, but that was all the more reason to treasure them. She couldn't have tolerated living with some volatile hothead always flying off the handle any more than she could have respected a man who never stood up to her. Star's timing was so precise; he knew exactly when to intervene. She had to smile.

"Oh, come now, it wasn't that bad, was it?" she said.

"You didn't have to sit with him in the living room before the meal, watching him squirm. If you had, you'd have thrown the pie at him, just to get him out of the house."

"I felt like throwing it at you."

Star smiled.

"Anyway," Sharon said, "it may not have been the

best Thanksgiving a family ever had, but it was a beginning. You will admit that."

"I don't know," Star said, glancing back at the yard. "I don't know if I can take this every year."

Then they went inside together and finished their meal in the peace and quiet to which, over the years, they'd grown accustomed.

Russian Agents On The Chesapeake Bay

Baiting ducks, before it was outlawed, had a long and honored history on the Chesapeake Bay. Even after it was outlawed it had a fairly long history, thanks to the efforts of such men as Lester Harmon and his good friend, hunting companion and possible slight relation, Carter Dewhart.

Carter Dewhart was a tall man of erect, regal bearing, with bright blue eyes, graying hair, and the same weathered, leathery complexion as Lester's. He was quite religious in the conventional sense (as opposed to Lester's ongoing feud with the Lord) and locally was so well respected, he was sometimes referred to as the "Salt of the Earth." He and Lester both knew that baiting ducks was a crime, but neither believed it was a sin. And if their friend C.E. Lee had got himself in trouble baiting ducks, it was not because he baited, but because he baited in excess. Carter and Lester baited in moderation. There was a big difference, if not in the eyes of the law, certainly in the eyes of the Almighty.

This morning Lester and Carter were setting up on the lee side of the sand point, a slender spit that extended a quarter of a mile out into the creek. Carter had a varicose leg. So while Lester put out the decoys, Carter busied himself on shore tidying up the blind.

Lester scattered twenty blackneck decoys to the incoming ducks left of the blind and a dozen jinglers, also know as goldeneyes, to the right. The idea was for the real ducks to land between the two groups of decoys.

When he finished putting out the decoys, Lester hid the skiff in a tall stand of sea oats about two hundred yards down the beach from the blind. He covered his ten quart bucket of corn with a burlap bag and shoved it under the bow. The corn would be for later. Lester never put the corn out until they had finished shooting, and he always stopped baiting a day or two before he planned to hunt. Knowing exactly when to quit required careful timing and the weighing of several factors, such as the size of flock, species, and who else was baiting. If you quit baiting too soon, the ducks would take their business elsewhere. Quit too late and you would be shooting over incriminating evidence.

When Lester arrived back at the blind, Carter Dewhart was pouring two cups of coffee from a corrugated aluminum Thermos. Carter provided coffee and conversation. Lester furnished labor and materials.

The morning sky was a dense grey canopy stretched from one horizon to another. A northeast wind spit snow that pinged off the men's oilskin hoods like birdshot. It was a perfect morning for ducks, and yet the sky was empty, as it had been more often than not for quite a few years.

At one time ducks had been so plentiful they had been harvested like a crop, trapped or shot, packed into barrels like potatoes and shipped north, redheads for fifty cents a pair, canvasbacks for seventy-five. Even after the market hunting ended and seasons and limits were established, sport hunting held up for many years. Then more and more people up North started draining marshes where the ducks bred, and plowing and planting the reclaimed land. So what you ended up with was an excess of wheat and a shortage of ducks. Which meant even shorter seasons and stricter limits in the South. But no one ever suggested re-flooding the marshes. No. Instead what happened was, the government bought up the surplus wheat, sold it to the Russians, and used the profits to pay for more game wardens down South — in rubles! At least that was how Lester heard it from C.E. Lee. He believed it too; he knew it for a fact.

Just as Lester was finishing his coffee, a small flock of buffleheads came into the creek from the right. They didn't ever used to shoot buffleheads — there wasn't much more meat on one than on a quail — but now that's about all there was to shoot. The ducks skirted the decoys, then veered downwind. At the far end of the creek, at the cove near Lester's house, the flock turned and dropped lower.

"I think this bunch just might do it," Carter Dewhart said. He had his hand on his gun.

The flock cut one way, then the other.

"First they got to talk it over," Lester said.

"I think they've decided in our favor," Carter Dewhart said.

Now the ducks had their wings set; they were dumping air. Then their legs came down. There was a point just before they would have pitched, when they were almost suspended in the air. That was the time to shoot. Lester and Carter Dewhart, without speaking, rose together and rattled off six shots so quickly the shots made the sound of one steady roar that echoed for several seconds back and forth across the creek. Five ducks fell.

"I couldn't catch up to that last one," Carter Dewhart said.

"I better get after those cripples," Lester said. He crawled out the back of the blind and walked quickly down the beach towards the skiff.

Three ducks were killed outright; a fourth could barely move, but the fifth could do everything but fly. He made a series of long dives aimed at the far shore. When he came up for air, he showed only a sliver of back and a slight bulge of head held low to the water, a silhouette barely detectable in the choppy sea. Lester hated chasing cripples around that creek, with all the new houses along the shore and all the city

56

people sitting at their windows with binoculars, all pulling for the duck. It was like hunting in an arena. He could feel a hundred eyes on his back. It was fifteen minutes before Lester finally ended the chase with a single shot that even in the wind sounded too loud.

When he was two hundred yards from shore, a small float plane passed low over the pines to the south, swung directly into the wind and landed on its first approach. A uniformed man hopped out onto the pontoon and lowered a dredge to check for corn, while the pilot taxied the plane through the gap in Lester's decoys right up to the beach. Lester guessed that would be the last time he used that particular pattern of decoys.

Lester's first inclination was to hold his course and return the skiff to the tall grass and find a better place for his bucket of corn than the bow of the boat, but before he reached shore, the agent on the pontoon was motioning for him to come there. Then the other agent was on the beach seconding the motion.

When Lester arrived at the beach, Carter Dewhart was just emerging from the blind, moving slowly down to the water's edge, his limp more noticeable than ever. He and Lester exchanged quick, criminal glances. The two wardens, a heavier, older one, and a younger, thin one, were both wearing dark green uniforms and green hats with no bills and fur ear flaps folded over the top. Just like the North Koreans wore, Lester noted.

"Right rough morning to be flying around, isn't it?" Carter Dewhart said.

"A little bit," the older heavier agent said.

"What can we do for you boys this morning?" Carter said.

"Aw, I don't know," the heavier one said. "I guess as long as we're here, we might as well check your licenses."

Lester handed over his license without a struggle. He thought he could smell vodka on the agent's breath, and the man spoke with a funny accent that sounded like it might have come from a language tape. The other one probably didn't even speak English.

"Where're you from?" Lester said, none too friendly.

"Fredericksburg," the senior agent said without looking up.

"I didn't think you were from around here."

The agent gave him a funny look. "It's not more'n sixty miles as the crow flies."

"I know where it is," Lester said. It was closer to Washington, D.C. than it was to his house. A lot closer.

The agent handed them back their licenses. "I see you boys are using automatics," the agent said, after he finished with the licenses. "What's that you've got there he said to Lester, "a Remington 1100?"

"Whatever it says on there," Lester said. He wasn't helping anybody arrest him.

"You don't mind if I check the plug, do you?"

Reluctantly, Lester handed the agent his gun.

While that agent checked the guns, Carter Dewhart chatted with the other one about his airplane, how fast would it go? How much room did it need to take off and land? And so on and so forth. Lester didn't join in the conversation. All he wanted to know about their airplane was how many rounds of heavy loaded number fours it would take to sink the son of a bitch.

He figured two rounds in each pontoon and those boys would be walking back to Moscow.

After the agent shucked the three shells out and reinserted them, he turned to Lester. "Could I have one of your shells?"

"What for?" Lester said. "It won't hold but three."

"That's right, Cap'n," Carter Dewhart said. "It's against the law for a gun to hold more'n three shells."

"I understand that," the agent said, "but we're required to check anyway."

"Of course, you are," Carter said. He handed the agent a shell, which he tried unsuccessfully to shove into Lester's gun.

"I told you it wouldn't go," Lester said.

When he finished both guns, the agent turned to Carter Dewhart. "You boys got a license for this blind, don't you?"

"Yes sir," Carter said. "You've got to have a license on a stationary blind. It's the law."

"You don't mind if Billy here checks, do you?"

"No, indeed. You go right ahead and make yourself at home. There's some coffee there if you'd like a cup."

"Thank you just the same."

Lester couldn't help but smile at "Billy." If that boy's name wasn't Vladimir, his wasn't Harmon. High cheek bones, squinty blue eyes, big dumb jaw.

The older agent noticed Lester's smile. "Something funny?"

"No sir," Lester said. He almost said "nyet."

"It's all right," Billy reported from the blind. Probably the only English phrase he knew, Lester figured.

"You don't mind if we look around a little bit, do you?" the heavier agent said.

"No, my word," Carter Dewhart said. "You tell us what you're looking for, we'll help you."

The agent said, "Well, you know how it is, sometimes a fellow will accidentally kill an illegal duck and feel so bad about it, he'll hide it in the bushes. Some others might hide a bucket of corn. We know you fellows wouldn't do that, but, like I say, they make us check everybody."

"We understand. You're just doing your job."

"That's it."

The one called Billy backtracked Lester's trail to where he originally hid the skiff, while the heavier one poked around closer to the blind, following a series of paths that radiated away from the blind like spokes of a wheel. Most led to places where Carter and Lester had, at one time or another, relieved themselves.

"Those two would make a right nice pair of bird dogs," Carter said.

"Yeah, That fat one's got a right good nose," Lester said. "For some things."

"Not very rangey, though."

"No, and he's not real stylish."

"Is that corn still in the skiff?"

"It's under the bow. You think they found anything with the scoop?"

"I believe they would've said something, by now, don't you?"

"I guess," Lester said.

When the two officers returned to the blind they both looked disappointed. "You mean to say you boys haven't killed a duck all morning?" the senior man said.

"No, indeed, we've killed ducks," Carter Dewhart said.

"Oh, well, why didn't you say so?"

"We thought you were only interested in illegal ducks, and all our ducks are legal."

"We have to check them all."

"They're in the skiff," Lester said. "I'll get them for you." His sudden cooperativeness struck a false note.

"Don't trouble yourself," the senior man said. "Billy will get them."

When Billy climbed into the boat and squatted down to examine the ducks, his rubber boots actually touched the burlap bag covering the bucket of corn. Lester's heart flapped against his chest like a trapped duck.

Billy shouted from the skiff. "Five bufflehead. Three hens and two drakes."

"Anything in their necks?"

"If there's any corn in them," Carter Dewhart said, "it probably came from back of the marshes. That's the direction they were coming from. I heard a terrific amount of shooting down there this morning. Sounded like a small war, didn't it, Les? Sounded like they had chosen up sides and were shooting at each other."

"The necks are clean," Billy said.

"They're probably from around here then," Carter said.

Then Billy climbed out of the skiff, and Lester's heart rate returned to normal. He was amazed. A child could have found that bucket of corn, but this pair of experts had missed it. He felt like pointing it out to them just to show them what fools they were. And to think he'd been so afraid of Communists.

"Well," the senior agent said, "it looks like you boys are all right this morning."

"And you'll find us to be all right each and every morning you check us too," Carter Dewhart said.

"Good, that's how we like to find people." He turned to leave.

"You ought to be ashamed of yourselves for even troubling us," Lester said.

The agent wheeled around. "I beg your pardon."

"The likes of you checking on the likes of us."

"Now listen here, you got no need to talk to us like that. We're paid to do a job, and we're..."

"I know you're paid," Lester said. "I know who pays you too."

Carter Dewhart came over and put his arm around Lester's shoulder. His hands were powerful from a lifetime of handling crabpots, trap stakes and oyster tongs. He drove his thumb into Lester's shoulder, the one he knew was troubled by bursitis. "Ow," Lester said.

"Officer, he doesn't mean any harm," Carter said in a voice so soothing it seemed impossible to be coming from the same person who was applying such painful pressure to Lester's shoulder. "No need to take offense. You have to understand, some people strive so hard to live an upright life, that when they're accused of doing..."

"We're not accusing any body of anything. This was just a routine check. That's all in the world it was."

"We understand that."

"We know you Harmons are good people..."

"The best there is," Carter said. "Proud people,

maybe a little too proud sometimes."

Lester felt another stab of pain in his shoulder.

"And Dewharts too, and you fellows shouldn't be taking this personally."

"And we don't either."

Lester took it personally. He took it very personally, but the agents were leaving. They were walking down to the plane, and he knew Carter Dewhart was right. There was no point provoking them now. Besides, you couldn't afford too much righteous indignation when you had a bucket of corn stashed under the bow of your skiff.

The plane taxied downwind, then turned and came rushing back towards the sand point. "Make a right easy shot," Lester said.

"You been spending too much time with C.E. Lee, that's your problem."

Lester's response was lost in the roar of the engine as the plane passed directly overhead and disappeared in the eastern sky. Carter put both guns in the blind, while Lester hid the skiff back down the beach.

Lester could see where Billy had trampled the vegetation, dug around in the sand, uprooted plants. The place had been invaded. Maybe Carter Dewhart was right. Maybe Lester did spend too much time with C.E. Lee, but C.E. Lee had a way of being right even when he was wrong. Maybe those agents weren't Russians, real Russians, but they might as well have been.

Lester knelt down on the beach and smoothed the sand and tried as best he could to straighten the bent and broken stalks; he replanted the ones that had been uprooted. Then he brushed the sand from his oilskin pants and walked slowly back up the beach to the blind, where Carter Dewhart was waiting with a cup of coffee.

One That Got Away

That winter the Northern Neck was almost over-run by geese. Every day large flocks moved back and forth between the grainery to the south and the vast fields of winter wheat behind the marshes, a flight path that carried them directly over Muddy Creek, but at such an altitude as to make hunting them seem futile, unless you were thirteen — almost fourteen — and thought your uncle, Lester Harmon, could perform miracles.

Lester was sitting beside the woodstove dabbing at the pipe he'd recently taken up to cut down on cigarettes. Roy was pacing back and forth across the worn green linoleum of Lester's kitchen. The sound of the geese made Roy restless. Lester didn't seem to notice. "Don't you hear them?" Roy said.

"I hear them," Lester said.

"Well?"

Lester listened for a minute. "Sounds like they're heading up back of the marshes."

"But they're passing right over Muddy Creek."

Lester sucked on his pipe and shook his head. "They're just traveling. About the only way to get a shot at a flock like that is from an airplane."

Roy went over to the mantle and for about the fourth time that afternoon studied the faded photographs of ducks and geese and quail that had been taken around there over the years. Then he went back to the window and watched another flock pass high over the lower field, a loose V that gradually disappeared into the grey sky. "O.K.," Roy said, "You can take that attitude if you want, but if you don't mind, I'd like to borrow your skiff and decoys."

Lester looked long and hard at his beloved nephew, then outside at the freezing rain falling on the hood of his car. He sighed, set his pipe down on the mantle, and put on his hunting clothes.

Lester's father, Luther cut the ditch between Muddy Creek and the bay. He was going to open Muddy Creek to oystering. There the oysters would be safe from storms and oystermen from Maryland. But the oysters didn't do well. They would grow, but there was no natural strike. By the time the Harmons realized the project was a bust, the ditch had washed and widened to where it had been declared a natural waterway. It was illegal to close it. And except for being straight, it looked like a natural waterway:

66

vines and trees along its banks, wading birds in its shallows, fish and crabs passing back and forth with the tides — and wooden skiffs laden with goose decoys and hunters either hopeful, or resigned more or less to their fate.

In Muddy Creek Lester started throwing decoys out with what looked to Roy to be reckless abandon, a totally random pattern. But every time Roy threw one out, Lester would patiently paddle over and move the decoy a few feet one way or the other, as if Roy had disrupted some precise pattern known only to Lester.

On shore they built a crude blind from cedar and bayberry branches. Each branch Roy placed Lester repositioned, always without a word of explanation. Inside the blind, Lester inspected Roy for any telltale sign of white, and finding a thin rim of exposed tee shirt, buttoned Roy's shirt collar for him. "I can dress myself," Roy said. "I'm not three years old any more."

"I know you're not. I was just trying to help. Now why don't you sit over there," he said, motioning to an upturned metal bucket. "I'll keep watch."

"Yes, Sir," Roy said as if addressing a superior officer.

Freezing rain sheathed the leaves in ice. When jostled, they made a noise like chimes, barely audible to Roy, but apparently much louder to his uncle. "Try not to move around too much," Lester said.

"I wasn't moving. I was shivering."

"Well, try not to if you can help it."

Roy looked at his uncle standing there in his dripping green oilskins, face grizzled and lined like a frozen leaf. He looked more like a natural object than a person. Roy wondered if he would ever really understand the man. Sometimes he treated Roy like an equal; other times he was like a tyrant. And Roy never used to have to push him to go hunting or fishing; just the opposite. He asked his mother about it once. She said Lester had "funny ways" about him. When he asked what she meant, she said sometimes he could be a little "peculiar." That was a big help.

Gradually the cold from the ground seeped up through the metal bucket into Roy's rear end, then moved like rigor mortis down his legs. He tolerated it as long as he could, but finally, when he couldn't take it any more, he pulled himself to his feet with the fragile branches of the front of the blind, which pulled loose from the shallow sand and ended up in Roy's hands like a pair of crutches.

"What the devil are you doing?" Lester said.

"Fixing the front of the blind," Roy said. "What does it look like I'm doing? You could see right through it."

"I didn't notice anything."

"Probably couldn't see it from your angle."

Roy took as long as he could repairing the blind. He positioned and repositioned the branches as carefully as if he'd been arranging flowers for an exhibition. When he was done, he stood there for a while longer stretching his legs. Finally, Lester said, "I guess you better let me do the looking."

"Awright," Roy said.

"Why don't you take that burlap bag and put it over the bucket. It might be more comfortable."

"That sounds like a good idea," Roy said. He folded the bag over the top of the bucket and sat down.

One "peculiar" thing Roy noticed about his uncle was his memory. His memory was unreliable.

Two summers earlier, one hot August night, he and Lester had fished until almost midnight on the grassy flats back of Lester's house for striped bass. There was a high tide and a moon so full they could tie knots and untangle line without using a light. The moonlight made the fish in the bottom of the skiff — and there were many fish — look like silver bars, like a treasure they had pulled from the bay. It was one of the nicest nights of Roy's life, one he knew he would never forget no matter how long he lived, or how old he got. Yet a few months after the fact, Lester had forgotten it entirely — the fish, the moon, the soft night air — it was gone. At first Roy thought Lester was teasing him; then he felt betrayed. How could he have forgotten such a night? Roy didn't understand it, but he decided, whatever happened, it wasn't Lester's fault, and also that he, Roy, could fix it.

So he set about to restore that night to Lester's memory. He told him the whole story over again, starting with the wind (a light southerly breeze), because Lester always started his own stories with the weather, and he told him the exact course of their drift, and what they used for bait (cut soft crabs), and how the moon looked on the water (like a piece of white silk, so real Roy felt like he could have picked it up and folded it and carried it home under his arm) and so on and so forth until Roy reached the part in his story where the largest fish of the night, a striped bass of about six pounds, took Lester's bait on the run, wrapped his line around the lower unit of the outboard, and just as Lester was about to net the fish, snapped the line.

"Daggone it," Lester said, when he heard that part. "You ought to have had the engine raised up."

"What?" Roy said. He couldn't believe Lester was blaming him for losing a fish that a few minutes earlier he hadn't even known existed.

"There wasn't any point in having the engine down if we were drifting, was it?"

Roy didn't say anything.

"Who was running the engine?"

"None of your damn business," Roy said, running from the house.

When his mother finally pried the story out of him, she said, "Oh, Roy, don't you see. That was Lester's way of thanking you. That was his way of telling you that fish hadn't really been lost. It had been, but you gave it back to him. I bet he can see that fish just as plain as you can now. He was trying to say thanks."

"Well, he ought to find a better way," Roy said.

"I'm sure Lester knows that," his mother said. "I'm sure Lester realizes that better than anyone."

Eventually the rain soaked through and froze the burlap bag. "Jeez," Roy said. "This wasn't such a great idea."

"What's the matter?"

"The darn bag is frozen."

"That won't hurt anything."

"Yeah, right, you're not the one sitting on it."

"It wasn't my idea to come, you know," Lester said.

"Nobody's blaming you either, O.K.?"

"Awright. But we can go any time you want to."

"I do not want to go. O.K.?"

"O.K., whatever you want to do."

Roy knelt in the frigid sand. The cold quickly penetrated his thin rubber hip boots. He thought he could feel the liquid of his knees congeal. He knew he'd never walk upright again.

"See anything yet?" he said a few moments later.

"No, nothing yet."

"Maybe I ought to look. Maybe I'd see something."

"Hush a minute," Lester said.

"What?"

"Hush!"

"Jesus!"

"SSssh," Lester said. "Don't move. Don't even breathe."

Roy actually drew in a breath, held it a few moments, then felt foolish and released his breath — too loudly to suit his uncle.

"How the devil do you expect to get a goose when you're keeping up such a racket?" Lester said in a loud whisper.

"You're making more noise than I am fussing at me," Roy whispered back. "No damn geese coming in here anyway."

Then Lester reached inside his oilskin jacket for the goose call, and that was when Roy finally heard what Lester had been listening to all along: a faint, distant, intermittent honking. Roy turned, parted the brush behind him and peered out into the grey sky above the bay. After several minutes of straining his eyes, he saw the two tiny specks — geese! — but so high he almost laughed out loud when Lester put the call to his lips and honked several times. The geese kept flapping slowly, steadily towards the marshes.

Then Lester blew three more times, this time louder, more insistent, more of a command than a request: Come. Here. Now. The geese slowed and seemed to look around at the vast expanse of bay and marshland beneath them, but did not alter their course. The next three calls sounded angry, a father's final warning before sending a disobedient child to bed without his supper. (Roy was glad to hear that tone of voice directed at something other than himself for a change) This time the geese slowed, turned and circled back towards the creek, but at the same improbable altitude.

Lester crouched down beside Roy, but kept his eyes on the geese. The geese still seemed too high to Roy to be taken seriously, but the way Lester worked his safety back and forth caused Roy's hands to tremble.

The geese made several high circles above the creek. Then Lester placed the call to his lips and gave a soft word of encouragement, and the geese went into a steep spiraling glide that ended in the center of the decoys. They landed with a loud splash, then sat there suspiciously eyeing their companions.

"You take the one on your side," Lester whispered.

Roy nodded.

"Now," Lester said.

"Now?"

"Now!"

Roy shoved his gun through the front of the blind and fired. His and Lester's shots hung in the air several seconds and even longer in Roy's ears. One goose paddled in aimless circles. The other was perfectly still.

Lester stood and ejected the spent shell from his

gun. "Some people say it's not sporting to shoot them on the water like that, but the way I see it, if a man wants sport with a shotgun, he ought to take up skeet." He sounded like he was quoting scripture.

Roy stood beside his uncle. His knees felt surprisingly normal. In fact, he couldn't remember when they felt quite so well. "The only thing I don't understand," Roy said, "is, once you had them on the water, why didn't you just swim them over to the blind. We could have wrung their necks and saved on gunshells."

"I didn't think about that," Lester said, "or maybe that's what I would have done."

Roy led the way through the marsh grass to where they had hidden the skiff. Every two or three steps he looked back over his shoulder to make sure the two geese were still there. "You needn't worry about those two," Lester said. "They aren't going anywhere that we don't take them."

Later Lester stood beside the woodstove tinkering with his pipe. Roy stood beside the window looking out at the rain and the approaching darkness. The two geese lay in the entryway. When Lester finally got his pipe lit, he rocked back and forth on the balls of his feet as he often did when he was feeling well. "I guess all in all we had a right fair afternoon," he said. Roy didn't comment. "It's not often you get geese to decoy like that." Lester said. "More often than not they'll pitch out a ways and swim in. If they even do that." He looked at his pipe again. It wasn't burning properly; it rarely did.

Roy was looking at the geese. Lying there on the floor, they looked smaller than they had in the air, and less mysterious with their feathers wet and bloody. All their magic was gone. Sarge, Lester's English pointer, sniffed at them with all the curiosity he might have brought to a bag of groceries.

Lester had his pipe lit again. "They were young geese," he said, between puffs. "Still had their pin feathers. You couldn't fool an old goose like that. Or a flock of any size. Young and foolish is what they were," he said looking at his nephew. Roy was still looking at the geese, the first he'd ever killed. He felt differently from how he thought he'd feel.

Lester's pipe was out again. He poked at it one more time, shook his head, opened the woodstove with his foot and tossed his pipe and pouch of tobacco into the firebox. "That's enough of that foolishness," he said, pulling out a pack of Salems.

Roy turned just in time to see the pipe disappear into the stove. "What'd you do that for?"

"Tired of the darn thing, that's why. I gave that pipe every chance in the world. It didn't want to be smoked. That's all I can figure." He lit a Salem, inhaled deeply and released the smoke lovingly from his lips. "Now that's more like it," he said.

"What do you smoke for anyway?" Roy said.

"Because I enjoy it. Why else would a man smoke?"

"Beats me."

"What's bothering you anyway? Didn't you have a good time?"

"Nothing's bothering me."

"Because I had a good time. I had a fine time. I'm sorry if you got cold and wet, but that's goose hunting, and anyway it wasn't my idea to go."

"Nobody said it was."

"You practically forced me to go, but I'm glad you

did now. It was worth suffering just to see those two geese come falling out of the sky like that. That's a memory of a lifetime."

"I've heard that before."

"What's that supposed to mean?"

"Nothing."

"Naw, go ahead and say it."

Roy looked straight at Lester. "Awright. How long *do* you think you'll remember it?"

Lester was quiet. Roy could see his eyes change, and Roy was sorry he'd said anything.

Then Lester said, "Are you still fretting about that fish we lost last summer?"

Roy looked back at the geese. At that moment, if he could have brought them back to life, he would have. He would have held the door for them and watched with pleasure as they waddled out of the house and leapt into the air. "It wasn't last summer," Roy said still looking at the geese. "It was summer before last."

Lester thought for a moment. "Is that a fact? It's so fresh in my mind, it seems like yesterday."

"Bull," Roy said.

"What?"

"Bullshit, that's what." Roy turned and looked out the window at the trees in the yard. The wind had come around from the southwest; the rain no longer froze as it hit. For the first time he was glad they had lost that fish. No matter whose fault it was, he was glad it had gotten loose, because if it had died, it would have been for nothing, because Lester had forgotten it. The fish they were talking about now wasn't that fish, the real one, the one that had gotten away. The one they were arguing about was one Lester had taken not from the bay but from Roy's memory. Just like his mother said. He was glad she'd told him that too. Otherwise he might have really held it against his uncle. Now he'd try not to.

Roy picked up his gun and goose and walked to the entryway, looking at his feet. "Lester," he said, "I'm sorry I talked to you that way. Do you forgive me?"

"There's nothing to forgive," Lester said. "Just don't let your parents catch you talking like that."

"Don't worry. I'm careful around them. I guess I ought to start being careful around you too."

"I don't know," Lester said. "We get along all right most of the time."

"Yeah, I guess we do."

Halfway home the rain stopped, and a thin sliver of moon shaped like the blade of a scythe appeared now and then among the clouds. A flock of geese passed invisibly overhead, honking and honking. Roy's own goose, slung feet first over his shoulder, bounced softly against his back with every step he took. Roy liked how it felt against his back and could hardly wait to show it to his parents.

Otha's Ghost

Lester Harmon did not consider himself a racist, not by any means, but he had to admit, some colored people sorely tested his patience, and none tested it more severely than Otha Lee Taylor.

For fifteen years Lester had worked side by side with Otha, driving stakes, tarring and hanging nets, bailing fish, sorting crabs, sweating in the hot August sun, shivering in March rains. They'd shared secrets and they'd argued and they'd suffered one another's long stony silences. Over the years, Lester had come to trust Otha and rely on him. Then one December, despite Lester's warnings, Otha went back to dredging oysters up near the Potomac River, fell overboard and drowned.

They knew what day he drowned; it was cold but not rough. The dredge hung on the bottom and tipped the boat far over to one side. Before the captain could release the clutch, the dredge pulled free, and the boat rocked hard the other way. Otha lost his balance and went overboard. They knew who the captain was. He was a good man. That made it Otha's fault.

"If he could have stayed afloat two minutes, that boat could have swung around and picked him up," Lester said.

"Right hard to swim in oilskins," C.E. Lee said.

"You'd think a man who spent as much time on the water as Otha did could swim a stroke or two."

"That cold water probably stunned him."

"Two minutes!"

Lester and C.E. Lee were the only white people at Otha's funeral. They weren't altogether sober, but they were there. After the service Otha's widow, Hattie, came up and comforted Lester for his loss. "He just worked for me," Lester said.

Afterwards Lester didn't feel quite right about that remark, but what was he supposed to say? C.E. Lee was there, and Lester was embarrassed. And Otha wasn't family, and he wasn't really a friend. Whites didn't have colored friends. Otha worked for him; he was an employee. No, there was more to it than that, but he didn't know what you called it.

In the spring Lester hired three different men to take Otha's place. Not one lasted longer than a week. The first one drank too much. The second didn't drink, but didn't work much either, and the third, Albert, talked constantly. He didn't talk about normal things either such as fish and crabs and other watermen; he talked about "civil rights." That was the last thing Lester wanted to hear about. He didn't even know what they were. When Lester let Albert go, he told him he'd be better off — they all would be — if he spent less time worrying about civil rights and more time learning how to swim.

After that, Lester tried to fish the Mary V. alone. Fishing alone wasn't easy. It was a lot of work for one man. It was wearing Lester down. He wasn't sleeping well either. He was having bad dreams about Otha — his eyes sad and accusing, teeth shining like tombstones, lips round and rubbery as an inner tube, or a life preserver, which if a man couldn't swim, he ought to keep nearby, if he had any sense. That sort of carelessness made Lester angry. There was no excuse for it. "I'd like to see him one more time just to tell him how mad at him I am."

He sort of missed him too. He missed arguing with him while they fished the traps. It helped pass the time of day. Otha had liked to argue. He'd been good at it too. He read, and he kept up on things. In some ways he'd been a right smart man. In other ways not so smart, because it wasn't too smart to argue too well with the man you worked for, and sometimes Otha would sort of out-argue Lester, but not any more. Now he lost every argument. Lester tried to be fair about it too. He'd been around Otha so long, he knew how his mind worked, and he could pretty much imagine what Otha would have said in any situation. Lester did his best to fairly represent Otha's side of the argument, but Lester's side was always just a little more convincing. Lester won about sixteen arguments in a row. He supposed he should have known that, dead or alive, Otha wouldn't tolerate that for long.

One day as Lester was fishing his traps and putting the finishing touches on his latest victory, he heard a humming sound. At first he thought it was the wind, or the bow line rubbing on a trap stake, or even a croaker grumbling under water. But none of those could carry a tune, and Otha could. He was humming "That Old Rugged Cross," one of his favorites. Lester liked it too. He never told Otha, but he could always work a little harder when Otha was humming one of his gospels. Made him feel better, more like working.

"I always did like that song," Lester said, when Otha was done. "That Old Rugged Cross, a symbol of suffering and shame."

"Yes, suh, that's what it is, suffrin and shame, suffrin and shame."

Otha's voice sounded perfectly normal, deep, soft and gravelly.

"You sound all right," Lester said.

"Can't complain, can't complain, considering the circumstances," Otha said. "And how 'bout you Cap'n? You doing all right?"

"About fair," Lester said. "Working right hard, and not sleeping so well. Too hot to sleep, I guess."

"Something troublin' your mind, I'd say."

Lester put the dip net down. "Well, to tell you the truth, I've been a little put out with you."

"With me?" Otha said, sounding hurt and innocent.

"Hire out to another man, go off and get yourself

drowned, leave me without any help, leave your family like that — that's no way to act."

"No need to take it personal."

"Maybe not, but I sort of did anyway. I'd gotten right used to you."

"Well, Cap'n, you know there's two ways of looking at that. For instance, if you paid a man a living wage, he wouldn't have to hire out in winter."

"I paid you all right."

"All right nine years ago. Not one raise since."

"You never asked for one."

"Not a day went by I didn't ask for one, one way or another."

"I thought you were fooling with me."

"Course you did, 'cause that's what you wanted to think."

"Are you blaming me for what happened?"

"Naw, suh, I'm not blaming you. I'm just saying what's what."

"It sounds to me like you're saying if I'd paid you more, you wouldn't have drowned."

"I said no such thing."

"You might as well have."

"But I didn't."

This was upsetting Lester. He'd forgotten how sneaky Otha was. He didn't argue fair. He had a way of twisting words around, a way of getting you to say what was on his mind. Before Lester could figure out what to say, C.E. Lee pulled along side in the Jean to buy crab bait.

"What are you talking to yourself so much about?" C.E. said, tying the two boats gunnel to gunnel.

"Who said I was talking to myself?"

"Lips moving a mile a minute. Didn't even hear my engine."

"Not that it's any of your business, but I was talking to Otha Lee."

"Oh, Lord. Did he talk back?"

"Suppose I said he did?"

"Wouldn't be too surprised. Take more'n a drowning to shut that Negra up. You got any big bunkers? I don't want any more of those little ones that fall right out of the bait bag. Save those for Jeter."

"I'll look," Lester said, "soon as I finish bailing these fish."

That was the last he mentioned Otha. C.E. Lee didn't believe in the spirit world. Only spirits he believed in came out of a bottle, and Lester didn't feel like being laughed at. So he dropped the subject, sold his bait and said goodbye. But he was still troubled by his conversation with Otha. "Imagine Otha blaming me, after all I did for him."

That night Lester didn't sleep well. He was afraid to sleep. Several times he'd doze off, then catch himself and jerk awake. He smoked a cigarette; he almost never smoked in bed. Soon he got up, dressed, went downstairs, had a cup of coffee and a slice of dry toast. Then he walked down to the dock.

Otha was sitting on the gunnel drinking ice water out of a Mason jar, same as always. He looked a little pale, and his skin was puckered the way it gets after being in the tub too long, but otherwise, he looked all right. Lester had seen him look worse. Lester spoke first.

"I've been thinking about what you said."

"What's that, Cap'n?"

"I don't think you're being fair complaining about how I paid you. Maybe I didn't exactly give you a raise, but I gave you a bonus every Christmas."

"Preciate it too, 'deed I do. Bought myself a bottle of wine every year and had change left over."

"And any time we had extra good fishing, I paid you extra."

"Yes suh, I expect you did. Way I remember it, I worked extra too."

"I didn't have to pay you extra. I just did it out of the goodness of my heart."

"Yes suh, I understand that."

"So?" Lester thought he'd given a pretty good account of himself.

"I never said you weren't a good man, Mr. Harmon. You treated me better'n most white people treat colored around here."

"Darn right I did." Looked like another victory for Lester.

"Just the same, there's still a lot of hungry mouths to feed up my way."

"Well," Lester said, "you should have thought about that before you went off and got yourself drowned."

"I did. It's why I went."

This was getting nowhere. They were talking in circles. "What do you want from me anyway?" Lester said. "Why are you here? Why are you harassing me?"

Otha said nothing. He just looked at Lester. His eyes were huge, sad, and accusing, same as in the dream. Otha picked up a mop and began washing down the gunnel and humming, "Onward Christian Soldiers."

"Don't start that humming," Lester said. "I don't

want to hear any humming now."

"Don't work for you any more. Hums when I feel like it."

"Gotten right uppity, haven't you?"

"Don't mean to be." He kept on scrubbing, leaning into a place where a dead fish had gotten ground into the gunnel. "You're not keeping this boat clean like you ought to."

"She fishes just as well clean or dirty," Lester said. This was an old argument; he didn't want to get into this again.

"Right much boat for one man any how."

"Well, maybe I'll get some help."

"Haven't so far."

"I still might. You don't know. You don't know everything. You just think you do."

"Time you were slowing down anyway, Cap'n. You're getting on in years."

"Not that old."

"Naw suh, not that young either."

"What are you driving at anyway?" Lester didn't like the drift of this conversation.

"Big work boat like this'd bring a nice price. Nigh 'bout two thousand dollars, I'd say."

"It's not for sale."

"Two thousand dollars'd do a lot of good for my people."

Lester couldn't believe what he was hearing. "You want me to sell this boat and give the money to your family!?"

"Now that's an idea," Otha said. "Might help you sleep better too. Maybe we'd both rest easier knowing my family was cared for."

"That's blackmail!" Lester said.

"Naw suh, I'd say it's more like back wages. Don't come to much more'n two hundred dollars a year. That's not even a dollar a day raise. Don't sound like much to me."

"I never heard of such a thing!" Lester said. "In all my life." Lester was pacing back and forth on the dock.

"Well, don't do it if you don't feel like doing it," Otha said. "It's altogether up to you." Then Otha resumed humming "Onward Christian Soldiers," a very spirited version with a sort of martial beat. He shouldered the mop like a rifle and marched into the little cabin in the bow of the Mary V.

"Come back here," Lester said. "I'm not done talking to you yet." But Otha was gone, and Lester wasn't about to go into that cabin after him either. "Darn Negra!" Lester said.

It was about the most aggravating thing that had ever happened to Lester. Not seeing Otha's ghost. He half expected that. If you believed the Spirit of Jesus Christ was still alive in the world, as Lester did about half the time (his faith ran a fever curve: struck like malaria, departed in a cold chill), then it wasn't hard to believe in other spirits. What got Lester was, this spirit was blackmailing him, this man he'd trusted and tried to do right by. "Is this what they mean by 'civil rights?" Lester said. "Playing tricks on white people?"

The next day there were no fish in his Deep Hole net, not a one. Something had cut a big hole in the pound, and all the fish had escaped. Lester had never seen such a thing. "What the devil?" he said. The only thing that could cut a net like that was a big shark, but there weren't any big sharks in the Chesapeake Bay. Well, occasionally a bull shark would wander in from the ocean, strangle itself in a gillnet and get its picture in the Rappahannock Record. So Lester decided that must have been what happened, but the whole time he was mending net, he was cursing Otha.

On the way in, his engine conked out. He'd had engine trouble before, plenty of it, but he'd never had it cut out with no warning. "Must be the gas line," Lester said.

It was. It had come apart right in the center. He'd never seen that happen before. He used to keep an extra piece of tubing in the cabin. He looked but he couldn't find it. He didn't look long, though. It was hot and stuffy in the cabin, and messy — dirty rags, pieces of rope, spare wrenches, and there was a hornets nest in one corner, with hornets in it. Also, the place was haunted.

Lester sat on the bow in the hot sun and smoked a cigarette. There was no breeze, and the tide was slack; so he wasn't going any where. He just sat and smoked one cigarette after another and waited. "Hope you're happy now," he said, but Otha wasn't answering any more. Lester had a strange feeling he wouldn't be seeing Otha again, only his good works: broken gas lines and empty nets. He felt a cold chill, cold and familiar.

Soon C.E. Lee pulled alongside, as Lester had known eventually he would. "What the hell you doing?" C.E. said.

"Just passing the time of day," Lester said.

"I see that."

"Got anything I can use for a gas line?"

"No indeed."

"Then I guess you'll have to give me a tow."

"I guess I will."

While they were rigging up the lines, Lester asked if C.E. knew anybody looking for a used workboat.

"You're talking foolish now," C.E. said.

"Too much work for one man," Lester said. "Too much aggravation."

"Get some help."

"That's even more aggravation."

"There was a fellow from Reedville," C.E. said, straightening up, stretching his back. "A crab potter, asking about a boat." He gave Lester the man's name.

"Maybe I'll give him a call," Lester said.

"Then what?"

"Might do some gilling out of my skiff. Catch about as many food fish as I would in a trap anyway."

"Might, but what am I supposed to do for crab bait? You're the last trap fisherman on the creek."

"Buy frozen bait."

"I don't believe in frozen bait. Doesn't catch like fresh."

"I can't solve my problems and yours too," Lester said.

"Oughtn't to talk like that to a man who's about to tow you in," C.E. said.

"Don't guess I should."

"Might cut this line and set you adrift."

"Wouldn't be the first time that happened."

That same evening Lester called the man from Reedville, and bright and early the next morning he was there to look at the boat.

"She's solid as a rock," Lester said. "She's just too

much for me. I've gotten a little too feeble to fish her any more." He bent over and limped around as he showed the boat.

He didn't mention Otha's ghost. No need to. The man didn't ask. If the man had asked if the boat was haunted, Lester wouldn't have lied. He would have said, yes, it was, a little bit in the cabin. The rest of her was all right. But the man never asked.

The day after he got paid, Lester carried twenty crisp one hundred dollar bills in an envelope to Otha's widow, Hattie, a frail, elderly woman. She met Lester outside her trailer and led him over to the sparse shade of a flowering mimosa. Otha's grandchildren played on the bare ground around them.

"How you doing this day, Mr. Harmon?" Hattie said. She sounded genuinely concerned for him.

"Doing about fair," Lester said. "I brought you something."

"I see you did."

He handed her the envelope. She peeked inside, then quickly shut the envelope and looked away.

"Now I don't want you getting overly excited about this," Lester said. He'd heard Otha speak of his wife's weak heart many a time, suspected it was a play for sympathy, but now he wasn't sure. "It's just some money I owed your husband."

"More'n 'some' money."

"Two thousand dollars," Lester said.

"Oh, my Lord," Hattie said, patting her chest.

Lester pulled a lawn chair into the shade, eased Hattie into it. Then he sat down beside her. "Now you put this money in the bank," Lester said. "You have a bank account?"

"Do now."

"Use it for necessities. Don't let the young ones get their hands on it. Fact, I wouldn't even mention it to them."

She shook her head. "No, my Lord. They'd throw it away."

"Probably be best if you didn't mention it to anybody. Just let it be our secret." The fewer people that knew about this, the better.

"Yes indeed, that's just what it is, our secret. Not anybody else's. And wouldn't anybody have known if you hadn't paid this money either. You're a good man, Mr. Harmon. Lord knows, you are, and I thank you."

"Well, I wanted to do what was right," Lester said. "Otha was a right good fellow.

"Deed he was, and I know you miss him too."

"In some ways I guess I do," Lester said.

Lester was chuckling as he walked back to his truck. It felt good to give that money away, but that's not why he was chuckling. He was chuckling because the joke was on Otha. Otha knew a lot about many things, but he didn't know much about the value of a good work boat. The fact was, Lester didn't sell it for two thousand dollars. He sold it for four thousand five hundred. He made more off the deal than Otha did. "And that Negra thought he was so smart," Lester said.

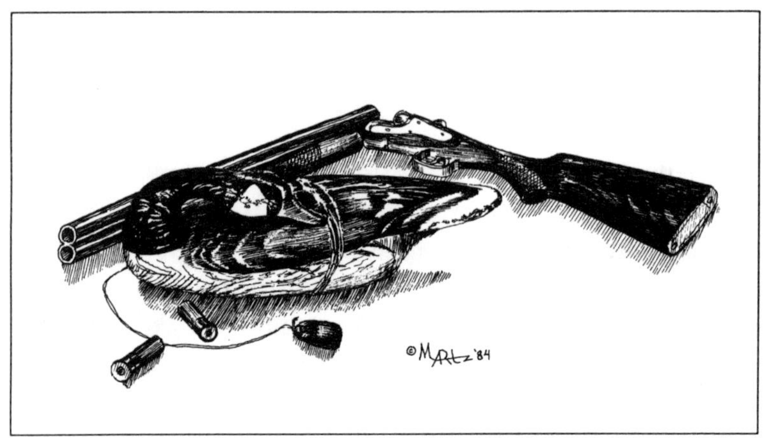

Parable

It was so cold in Lester's attic, where he was hanging a gill net, that he could see his breath. It was the coldest Christmas on record. The creek was frozen solid. You couldn't hunt ducks in this weather. You couldn't even oyster, but Lester didn't miss that the way he missed the ducks.

He put his net needle down, rubbed his hands together and blew on his fingers. He wiggled his toes and walked around on the warped plywood floor. Then he went to the window and picked up his binoculars. The lens fogged from the heat of his face. He wiped them with the sleeve of his flannel shirt and looked towards the creek. He could see Star and Sharon

Harmon's new house along the shoreline, and beyond that the sand point, and beyond the sand point the bay, where big flocks of diving ducks were rafted up in the open water. As he watched, a small flock of scaup — he could tell they were scaup by their acrobatic flight — circled the creek, dipping low in front of his blind where the corn lay locked under a layer of ice, then swooping up over the beach and disappearing out into the bay. He felt a longing as the ducks disappeared, sadness at the departure — an opportunity missed — and hunger. He loved the taste of wild duck. Then his glasses fogged again, and he thought, "This must be what it's like to have cataracts."

He went back to his net; the room seemed colder than ever. Those binoculars made him think. He'd known a woman once who had cataracts, a colored woman who lived in a trailer at the end of the tarred road. She was so blind her children used to lead her around the yard by the arm. Then one day she went to Richmond, and when she came back she could read newsprint. Well, he doubted she could actually read anything, but she liked to sit in the yard with a Times-Dispatch in her lap, showing off her new eyesight.

When he thought about her, it seemed like a parable, The Blind Woman and the Cataracts, like there was message in that story for him, same as in scripture. Soon he saw what it was: those ducks were blind, they could not see. The ice obstructed their vision. He saw at once what had to be done. "Son of a gun," he said. "The Lord sure works in strange ways." But why couldn't He be more straightforward, he wondered?

Lester dropped his net needle, scrambled down the attic ladder, got his hunting gear and gun and went outside. He found an old scaup decoy in the dock shed, shoved it into his game bag, grabbed an axe and headed up the road.

There was dusting of new snow over a crust of old snow, and fresh tracks of rabbit, squirrel, crow, and a cock pheasant. He could tell it was a cock by the tail mark between its feet. A hen's tail didn't reach the ground. Soon he came to the tracks of two humans on cross country skis. He could tell those by the endless parallel grooves, and the round regular pole marks, and here and there the deeper indentations of knees and elbows and the wider shallower depressions of buttocks. He had to laugh. No other animal left as much evidence in its wake as humans, and he doubted any other humans left as much as Star and Sharon Harmon, who, in what Lester thought might have been a murder-suicide pact, had given each other cross country skis for Christmas. The only thing that might save them was, most winters there wasn't any snow.

Where the road turned left through the lower field, the skier's tracks were so pockmarked and scarred, it looked like they'd been hit by an artillery barrage. The he saw Star and Sharon up ahead, taking a few cautious steps at a time, then collapsing in a pile of skis, poles, knees, elbows. From where Lester stood, it looked more like a nervous disorder than a sport. Just walking at his normal pace, he caught up to them in no time.

Star and Sharon were wearing knickers, knee socks and matching blue sweaters with white deer strung like paper dolls across the fronts. They were covered with snow.

"You'd make a lot better time, if you'd take those things off your feet," Lester said.

Star laughed, but Sharon said, "You ought to get yourself a pair of these, Lester. Be the best thing in the world for you."

"Looks too dangerous to me," Lester said.

"Not dangerous at all. What's dangerous is sitting inside all winter smoking too many cigarettes and eating too much rich food."

Lester patted his stomach. "All animals put on fat in the winter. It's natural." He didn't have any excuse for smoking, except he planned to quit. He was going to take up the pipe again. Fight fire with fire, that was the plan.

"Where're you going with that axe?" Star said.

"Going ducking."

"Going ducking? How the devil you going ducking with the creek frozen up?"

"I got a plan," Lester said. "Came to me in a vision."

"Oh, Lord, spare me," Sharon said. "What're you bothering the ducks for anyway? Don't you think they've got enough trouble finding food in this weather?"

"I'm going to make it easier for them."

"I bet you are."

"Hasn't it been cold, though?" Star said. "Have you ever in your life seen it so cold at Christmas time?"

"Well," Lester said, "now that you mention it..." He started reminiscing about some other memorable winters, one when Star was a child and still living on the farm. That was the winter when their Uncle Golden drove his car across the creek to Ditchley. That reminded Star of some other crazy things that Golden did, like putting in a ditch from Barnacle to Indian Creek. They talked about that for a while. Meanwhile, Sharon was getting restless. She began running her skis back and forth in their tracks, and then, when that didn't have any effect, she sighed a couple of times and finally got Star's attention. They exchanged looks and Lester said, "Well, I won't hold you up any longer. I've got to get going anyway. Darn days are so short."

"Well, it was nice chatting with you," Star said.

"Stop by sometime, Lester," Sharon said. "It's that time of year. Don't be such a stranger."

"Awright, maybe I will," Lester said.

The lower field ended in a three foot drop down to the beach. Every year the drop-off moved further back into his field, as more land washed into the bay. Fact was, the farm was shrinking. And yet, at the same time that was happening, his property taxes were going up. The way things were heading, one day someone was going to have to pay a fortune on a farm that didn't even exist. He was glad he didn't have children. Glad he didn't have a wife too.

He walked up the beach to his duck blind, a plywood box buried in the sand, surrounded by sedge grass and sea oats. He sat on an upturned fish box and smoked a cigarette and waited to see if any ducks would accidentally fly by close enough for him to get a shot without having to go through with the rest of the plan, which would mean walking out onto that ice, which didn't seem quite as inspired now as it did

94

when the idea first hit him. That ice didn't look so thick close up. Maybe he had misunderstood the parable. He went back over it again in his head.

No, he decided, he got it right: he was supposed to go out there and chop a hole in the ice. Then God would send in the ducks. He decided to smoke one more cigarette to see if maybe God wouldn't send in the ducks without the hole, but it didn't work. He knew it wouldn't work. He mashed his cigarette out in the snow and walked to the water's edge.

He tested the ice with his axe, until he came to a solid place. He stepped onto it, and the ice groaned. He poked along like a blind man with the axe in front of him. He felt blind, because the snow covered the ice, and he couldn't see the bad places. He had to feel for them, tap, tap, tap with the handle of the axe. He could see how it fit with the parable, but still he didn't like it. "I don't appreciate this," he said out loud.

He finally got far enough from shore, but he did not want to take that axe and chop into the ice that he was standing on. It was deep water there. "It's deep water here," he said. He could see that one whack and he might go straight to the bottom. Finally he lay down on the ice to spread his weight. He held the axe in front of him, raised it, and let it fall of its own weight onto the ice. Nothing. He had to get on his knees to get leverage to cut through the ice, which was three inches thick. He felt ashamed.

"I'm sorry I doubted You," he said. "I'm sorry." To make up for his weak faith, he made the hole twice as large as he had planned, and he did an especially neat job, rounded the edges, shoved the lose ice out of the way. Then he tossed in his decoy and walked quickly back to the blind.

He smoked a cigarette and waited. Then he smoked another cigarette. He looked all around for ducks, but the flocks that had been flying in one after another all afternoon were nowhere to be seen. Nothing. He felt like a fool. There he sat, just like that colored woman, fooling no one. Neither of them could read. "Nothing means anything," he said.

Then a big drake goldeneye flew into the creek and circled high overhead. Lester dropped to his knees and held perfectly still. He knew that duck would not come in, but if it didn't, it wouldn't be his fault. The duck flew way back into the creek, near Lester's house, then came barreling back out. Lester could tell the moment the duck saw the open water and the decoy. It made a quick little motion in the air, and then one smooth curve that carried him into the patch of open water Lester had made with his axe.

The duck dove to feed, and while the duck was under water, Lester raised his gun up and flipped the safety off. When the duck surfaced, Lester whistled. Alarmed, the duck raised his head. That was when Lester fired. Then he sat back on his fish box and smoked a cigarette. His faith had been vindicated. When he finished the cigarette, he knelt down in the sand and gave a prayer of thanks. "Amen," he said, and then as a sort of postscript, he added, "I don't mean to be critical, but it might help if in the future, You could be a little more direct in your communication." He knew he was pushing his luck, and sure enough, when he looked up, two seagulls were pecking away at his duck.

Seagulls! They saved the Mormons; now they had

come for his duck. Like hell they had. "You sons of bitches! Get away from there," he yelled. He would have shot them both on the spot, but it was a federal offense to shoot a gull, and those new houses had eyes and big mouths.

He ran out onto the ice waving his arms, until finally, at the last second, the gulls flew away. He picked up his duck and checked the damage. It could have been worse. A little breast meat was gone. That was about it. It could have been a lot worse. He took the duck back to the blind and laid it between his feet. "Try and get it now," he said.

His heart was pounding. It had been an exciting hunt. He didn't know what it all meant, but he was pretty sure it was another parable. He'd sort it out later. For the moment, he felt truly blessed, and he sat in the blind until dark rejoicing at his good fortune.

At dusk the lights came on in all the houses around the creek except Lester's. The gap of his house stood out like a missing tooth. "I should have left a light on," Lester said. All the other houses had Christmas lights. One house had a plastic Santa Claus with reindeer on the roof. Another had a cross of white lights. There was a Nativity scene in one yard with spotlights illuminating it from several directions. Star and Sharon had the cedar tree in their yard lit up and another tree inside by the picture window. Lester could see the shadows moving back and forth behind it in the soft colored lights. "Next year I'll decorate my house," he said.

When it was fully dark, he gathered up his gun, duck, axe and decoy and started up the beach and through the lower field in the moonlight. The snow was firm again and crunched noisily beneath his feet. A flock of ducks passed silently overhead, their wings flickering in the moonlight. He stopped opposite Star and Sharon's house and looked and listened. The sky was so full of stars it was hard to separate the horizon from the rooftops. He could hear Christmas music coming from his cousins' house. It filled him even more with the Christmas spirit. He reached back and felt for his duck, then pulled it from the game bag and studied it in the moonlight. He wiped the blood away from the duck's mouth and smoothed its feathers. "There's nothing in the world wrong with this duck," Lester said. And Star Harmon had always been right fond of wild duck. And Sharon herself said, "Don't be such a stranger. Stop by sometime." And they were always giving him things, and he never had anything to give them. And now he did. Something very special too, a Christmas duck.

They were playing "Hark, The Herald Angel Sings" when Lester stepped onto the porch, leaned his gun against the rail and rang the bell. Sharon answered the door and seemed startled to see a man holding a dead duck out to her. Her mouth opened a little. "I'll get Star," she said, before Lester had a chance to say anything. She shut the door, then, a few moments later opened it again. "Don't you want to come in?" she said.

"No, I can't stay'" Lester said. "I just brought you a little something."

Soon Star came to the door. He was wearing his maroon smoking jacket and slippers. "Well, hello, Les," he said. "Come on in and have some eggnog."

"Thank you just the same," Lester said, "but I can't stay. I brought you a duck."

"I see you did." Star stepped out onto the porch and shut the door behind him. "I see you did," he said again.

Lester held the duck out with both hands, stroked the breast feathers. "Gulls got to him a little bit, but they didn't do any real harm."

Star shoved up the sleeves of his smoking jacket and poked at the breast. "Right plump, isn't he?"

"Fat as butter," Lester said. "I don't see how they stay so well fed in this weather."

"What is it, a blackneck?"

"No, indeed. It's a drake jingler. Golden-eye's the real name, I guess."

"Hard to tell in this light. I heard you shoot. How many did you kill?"

"Just this one," Lester said. "Only one that came in. Tell you the truth, I felt right lucky to get this one."

"I guess you were, clever too, but I couldn't take your only duck, Les. I wouldn't feel right about it."

"I wouldn't have brought it to you if I didn't want you to have it," Lester said.

"I know you wouldn't have, and it's darn nice of you, too, but it wouldn't be right for me to take it. Not after you sat out there all afternoon in the cold and I was sitting in here around the fire."

"That doesn't matter. It's your Christmas present. It's all you going to get from me too, so you better take it. It's a right special duck, too."

"I'm sure it is, but you don't need to give us anything, Lester. We got more'n we need already."

"I want to give you something. I want to give you this duck. You used to be right fond of wild duck, as I remember."

"I guess I was at one time. Been so long I can hardly remember what it tastes like."

"A jingler can be fishy, but this one won't be. I guarantee that. This one's corn fed. Just soak him in a little salt water overnight. Then cook him in a covered pan with a some water for about three hours..."

Star shook his head, held up his hands. "I couldn't, Lester. I wouldn't feel right about it."

Lester didn't know why he was standing on that porch arguing with someone he hardly knew any more. "Well, I can't make you take it," Lester said.

He shoved the duck back into his game bag. Lester was starting to say goodnight when the door opened and Sharon moved in behind her husband. She had a small red package in her hand. She handed it to Star and he handed it to Lester. "Merry Christmas."

"What's that for?" Lester said. "You already gave me one package."

"It's just a little something we wanted you to have," Sharon said. "It doesn't amount to much."

"Awright," Lester said, shoving the package into his game bag beside the duck.

"Don't you want to come in and have some egg nog?" Sharon said. "I know you must be freezing."

"No. Thank you. I've got to be getting back. Sarge has been locked up all afternoon."

"Sometimes I think you prefer that dog's company to ours anyway," Sharon said.

"I wouldn't say that."

"She's just fooling," Star said. "Lester brought us

a duck."

"I saw he did. It was nice of him too."

"I told him we wouldn't think of taking his only duck."

"Of course, we wouldn't. As much trouble as he went to. "

"But I'll tell you what," Star said. "Next time you cook a duck, you give me a call. We'll have us a duck dinner at your place. I'll bring the beer and all the fixings. How about that?"

"Awright," Lester said. "If I think of it, maybe I will."

They said goodnight, and Lester walked slowly back up the road. "Maybe I should have picked it and cleaned it and wrapped it in cellophane," Lester said.

He stopped at the ditch that connected the bay with Muddy Creek, and stood on the bridge and looked down into the water. The tide was rising and the water swirled heavily around the pilings. It seemed strange to see open water when all the rest was frozen.

He stared into the swirling water for a long time. After a while he felt the corner of the small package pressing into his ribs. He removed it from his game bag and held it up in the moonlight. He turned it one way then the other, then shook it. "I wonder what the devil that could be," he said. Then he tossed it into the heavy current and walked quickly up the road to his house.

Close To Nature

Why would a grown woman want to go out gillnetting? That's what Lester couldn't understand. It wasn't the same as when he'd had the big boat and Evelyn was a little girl and would sit up on the cabin, safely out of harm's way. The big boat was gone; he'd told her that. Now she'd get her clothes dirty; now she'd smell like fish. "That's the whole idea," she said. She wanted to get her clothes dirty. She wanted to smell like fish. Why would a grown woman want to smell like fish? That's what Lester couldn't understand.

Lester was standing on the end of his dock smoking a cigarette. In the early morning light he couldn't see the other houses lining the cove. It was as if the whole place was his again. Then a light came on across the creek. Evelyn was up.

He flicked his cigarette into the water and loaded two bushel baskets and an extra tank of gas into his skiff. He had no idea where she'd sit. He'd removed the middle seat to make room for fishing gear. She'd need a fairly substantial place to sit. As he remembered, she was pretty wide in the hips. C.E. Lee once said, "Evelyn Harmon Hoyt is so broad abeam she ought to paint her name across her stern." C.E. Lee was often saying such things about women, usually his ex-wives, and Evelyn wasn't anywhere near as large as C.E. said, but she would need a sturdy seat. Lester doubted an upturned bushel basket would do the job. He found a fishbox that was rugged and fairly clean and set it upside down near the bow.

Then the light went off across the creek; a door slammed; a car engine started, revved, its sound sank into the distance, then was loud again in Lester's lane, then silent. Soon Evelyn came strolling down onto Lester's dock. "Don't you just love this time of day?" she said. "It's so quiet and peaceful."

"Should have been here a few minutes ago. It was really peaceful then," Lester said.

"Same old Lester," Evelyn said. She was wearing jeans and a T-shirt. She had cut her hair, but it was black as ever. And she'd put on weight, but still wasn't fat, just stocky. C.E. Lee once said that Evelyn was built more like a quarterhorse than a thoroughhred, and, as a matter of fact, all her marriages had been sprints.

Evelyn took a deep breath and let it out very slowly.

"This salt air is so wonderful. You can't get air like this in the city."

"You can take some back with you if you want," Lester said.

Evelyn climbed down into the skiff and stuffed a canvas bag under the bow. "I brought some beach things," she said. "I thought, if you didn't mind, you could drop me off on the sand point on the way back in. If it's not too much trouble."

"No trouble," Lester said." I can drop you on the way out, if you want."

"You haven't changed a bit."

Evelyn sat on her fishbox, and Lester pulled the starter rope. The engine fired on the first pull. He backed the skiff away from the dock through a cloud of fumes.

At the first channel marker, Evelyn pointed to a pair of nesting ospreys and looked back at Lester to make sure he had seen them too. She gestured just as enthusiastically to a flock of sea gulls perched on the sand point, as if they too were objects of great natural beauty, instead of, in Lester's opinion, seafaring pigeons. When the sun burned through the mist like a flame blazing through a pile of dried brush, Evelyn looked like she would burst.

Lester cut the engine at the downwind clump of Chlorox bottles he used as a buoy and worked some slack into the net. "You're lucky, you know that?" Evelyn said.

"How's that?" Lester said.

"To be able to work out here in such beautiful surroundings, so close to nature. Sometimes I feel like the city is destroying me."

"It's not always like this," Lester said as he was struggling to raise the heavy lead line. He didn't elaborate, but sometimes the bay was cruel and rough and cold. If you romanticized the bay, she'd kill you. She killed Otha, threw him overboard and drowned him. So don't tell Lester how lucky he was to work so close to nature. Tell Otha. You couldn't get any closer to nature than Otha was. He was part of it.

Lester pulled slowly, steadily down the net. A few spot appeared at irregular intervals, murky white forms near the leadline. In the fall, when the water was clear and cool, the spot would turn a deep rich yellow, and when the fishing was good, the leadline would glow like a gold necklace. That was pretty gilling. Lester wasn't denying there was great beauty in nature, but in his opinion, nature was most beautiful when she was made to do man's bidding. Lester had a working relationship with nature, and no question who was boss.

This was not pretty gilling. This was midsummer gilling, with hot, murky water, fish spoiling in the net, too many menhaden and crabs and, worst of all, the sea nettles that clotted the net in gelatinous globs, making it heavy for Lester to lift and easy for the fish to see. Underwater a clean net was all but invisible; a net full of sea nettles was like a wall of Jello.

Evelyn was soon restless and wanted something to do. Lester let her pull the top line, the corks. Most of the fish, being bottom feeders, gilled near the leads, which Lester was pulling. "That's not fair," she said. "You're getting all the fish."

"That's how it is some days," Lester said. "Some

days they gill high, and some days they gill low."

She seemed to believe him. Lester was amazed. Then a fish showed up on her side of the net. It was a croaker, also called "hardhead," because of its hard, sharp gill plates. "You better let me do that one," Lester said. "They can be right mean to get out."

"You just take care of your end of the net. I'll take care of mine." Evelyn struggled to free a strand of net that was embedded in a gill plate. When she tried to force it, the gill plate sliced her thumb. "Ow," she said. She shoved her thumb into her mouth.

"I told you those things were mean," Lester said. But when he reached over to take the fish, she pushed his hand away.

"I hope you don't think I'm giving up that easily," she said.

He let her have the fish. He didn't want to fight with her. She had a fierce determined look on her face, as if that fish meant a lot to her. Lester looked up at the sun. It had shrunk to the size of a quarter and glowed like molten silver. He wiped his forehead and looked off into the distance for the other buoy, then at his watch. At the rate they were going, the fish already in the boat would spoil before they reached the other end. He looked back at Evelyn. She was still struggling with the same mesh.

"Just break the darn bar," Lester said.

"What?"

"Just break that one mesh that's holding it."

"Oh, why didn't you say that sooner?"

"I don't like to break any more than I have to."

Evelyn tried to break the strand of net, but couldn't get her fingers under it well enough to apply pressure.

"That monofilament is right rugged stuff," Lester said. "Not like those old cotton nets."

"It's not that tough," Evelyn said. "I just can't get a grip on it."

When she tried to reposition the fish, it drove the spines of its dorsal fin into the heel of her hand. "Damn it!" She dropped the fish and placed her hand back into her mouth.

Lester reached over and snapped the strand of net as if it had been sewing thread. The fish flopped around on the bottom of the boat. Evelyn kicked it towards the stern. "Be careful," Lester said. "Those spines will go right through a tennis shoe."

While Evelyn licked her wounds, Lester pulled as quickly as possible down the net. He wasn't glad she got hurt, but if she did have to get herself hurt, he was grateful for the location of the wound. With her hand in her mouth, she couldn't talk or help. But Evelyn wasn't that easily defeated. Soon she was bored and restless again.

"There must be something I can do," she said.

"Not really," Lester said. "Gill netting is pretty much a one man operation. I told you that."

"I can at least bail the boat out," she said. Several inches of sea water and fish slime had accumulated in the bottom of the boat. "Haven't you got a scoop?"

He tossed her the cut up plastic milk carton he used as a scoop. He was about to warn her to be careful of the sea nettle juice that mixed with the sea water, when he felt a heavy throbbing far down in the water and forgot about Evelyn.

When small fish such as spot gilled, the net usually closed their gills and killed them. But a fish too large to gill would tangle a corner of its mouth in one mesh and stay alive, and only lightly held by the net. What Lester felt was large and very much alive. He knelt down and peered into the water to see which side of the net the fish had hit. He raised the net very gently until the pale outline of a large grey trout came into view. Lester formed a sort of hammock around the fish, and eased the trout — six or seven pounds — into the skiff. When he flipped the net over, the fish fell out of its own weight and began thrashing wildly about in the bottom of the boat towards Evelyn.

"I'll get him for you," Evelyn said. She reached for the fish, and the swish of its tail sent a shower of sea water and slime into Evelyn's face.

"Jesus!" she said covering her eyes with her hands.

Lester came forward, shoved his fingers into the trout's gills, and slung the fish into a bushel basket. "Put some water in your eyes. That's the only thing that'll take the fire out. Bay water."

"Don't worry about me, O.K.? I can take care of myself."

Lester returned to the stern and began pulling along the net. "Those darn sea nettles are the dickens anyway," Lester said. "Otha used to say that one day a man would find a use for sea nettles, and then we'd all..."

"Lester !"

He was quiet for a while. If she didn't want to know what Otha said about sea nettles, then to heck with her. He wasn't glad she'd gotten sea nettle juice in her eyes. He wouldn't wish that on anyone. But maybe now she'd look at things a little differently. Maybe sea nettle juice in her eyes would improve her vision.

When Evelyn's eyes stopped watering, she sat on her fish box and watched, but Lester could tell she was getting restless again. After a while she reached up and took the top line. "I can at least do this much," she said.

He didn't argue. He was tired of trying to save her from herself. Soon a huge tangle of net came on board. In the center of the gnarl was a hard crab eating a dead fish. The tail had been cleaned to bone. "It's an amazing thing to me," Lester said. "His predicament hasn't even fazed his appetite. I've seen it many a time, and it never ceases to amaze me."

"What are you talking about?"

"There's no way he's getting out of that mess alive. Yet he just keeps right on eating. I guess there's a lesson in that, but darned if I know what it is."

"What do you mean he won't get out alive?" Evelyn said, pulling the net her way.

"You won't get him out in one piece." Monofilament had a way of hanging in the crevasses of the crabs legs and on the sharp edges of its shell.

"That's what you think," she said. "This is one thing I'm good at, messes!"

Evelyn evidently had taken Lester's statement as a challenge, though he hadn't meant it as one, and she plunged into her work with grim determination. Lester sighed and sat down on the gunnel and lit a cigarette. "Even if you can get him out, it'll take too long. You spend ten minutes on every crab, and all your fish'll spoil before you get in."

"You just hold your horses."

Lester looked off into the bay. A couple of crab potters, a few sport fishermen, and not a fish trap to be seen. A sad sight. He never thought he'd see the day.

Evelyn was down to the last layer of net holding the big male crab. Its pincers were clamped tightly shut on the dead fish. The crab's eyes pivoted on little turrets; foam oozed from its mouth.

"You be careful," Lester said. "A Jimmy crab that size can break a finger."

"Thanks, that's just the sort of encouragement I need." She struggled with a strand of net caught in a leg joint. Her hands were shaking slightly. Lester wiped his forehead and looked at his watch. "Just be patient," Evelyn said. "I won't be long."

The crab released the fish with one claw, snapped at Evelyn. "Stop it, you stupid thing. I'm on your side."

"Let me show you how I do it," Lester said.

"Just hold on. I'm doing all right."

She began talking to the crab in a soothing tone of voice, trying to persuade it that she understood its predicament. She even stroked its shell; the second time she tried, the crab clamped down on her thumb. "Ow!" she yelled and ripped her thumb free, tearing the skin.

Lester pulled the tangle of net his way. "Here's how I do it," he said, centering the crab on the gunnel and placing the heel of his boot on the back of the crab's shell.

"No!," Evelyn said, as the shell shattered with a loud crack.

Lester ground the crab into mush, then dropped the net overboard. Pieces of crab drifted off in a yellow stain, and the net slowly unraveled and sank.

Evelyn shook her head back and forth; she was crying. "I almost had it," she said. "I could have worked it out. All I needed was a little more time. Why'd you have to kill it?" She turned and faced the other way. "So cruel."

Lester didn't know what to say. He'd never seen anybody get that upset over a crab before. If he'd known it meant that much to her he wouldn't have crushed it. He didn't know she'd grown so attached to it or he wouldn't have killed it. "There'll be more crabs," he finally said. "The bay's full of crabs. Otha used to say winter dredging would ruin the crabbing, but..."

"Please!" Evelyn whispered.

Lester was silent for a while. He knew he shouldn't have brought her. She had been away too long. She'd spent too much time in the city. Here she was in the restaurant business — she'd probably served more crabs than he'd ever caught — crying over one crab!

When he was nearly at the end of his net, Lester felt a heavy throb. He hoped for another big grey trout, but it was a dog shark. He pulled the dull grey fish quickly in. Normally he'd take a dog shark by the tail, slam its head against the side of the boat and watch it swim off upside down, but he handled this one like a baby, and released it alive. "I don't think he's any worse for the wear," he said .

At the end of the net Lester let the boat drift in the breeze. He washed his hands overboard, peeled his oilskins down and shook a cigarette from its pack. As he leaned back against the outboard and smoked his cigarette, he looked at his hands, which burned where the salt water had hit the many cuts and scrapes. His hands were a mess. They looked like a pair of worn out leather gloves. If they hadn't been attached to his wrists, he'd have thrown them out.

Evelyn was still turned the other way when she started talking. "Do you remember when I used to go out fishing with you when I was little?" she said without turning around.

"Sure I do," Lester said. "You used to go out with me a lot."

"Almost every morning some summers. You were fishing traps then. I used to ask you so many questions I'm surprised you didn't throw me overboard."

"You weren't that much trouble," Lester said. "Not the way I remember it."

"You know, looking back, I think those were the happiest days of my life. That's sad, isn't it?"

"I don't know if it is or not," Lester said. "Those were right good times. I don't know if I've had any better ones myself."

"But that's different!" Evelyn said, turning now and looking straight at Lester. "You're a commercial fisherman. I'm a business woman. I'm thirty eight years old. I've been married. I've been a lot of things. And to look back over my life and realize that the happiest time was when I was ten years old, on a goddamn fishing boat..." She shook her head. "It's tragic. No, no that's too big a word for it. It's pathetic, that's what it is. Pathetic."

She looked like she was going to cry again, and Lester didn't know what to say. So he just cranked the engine. "These fish are going to go soft if I don't get them on some ice soon," he said. Then he threw the engine into gear and headed for the sand point. To see where he was going he had to look past Evelyn, who was still staring at him. Soon she turned and looked inshore.

Lester cut the engine in the shallow water. Evelyn tossed her bag up onto the beach, then hopped overboard and held the bow of the skiff offshore so it wouldn't rub. She seemed to be feeling better. "I'm sorry if I loused up our morning," she said.

"You didn't hurt anything. I'm sorry you didn't have a better time."

"It was fine. I've just lost my touch with fish."

"You can go with me tomorrow if you want to."

"That's nice of you, but I don't guess I will."

"Suit yourself. Are your eyes all right?"

"They're fine. Hands too. Superficial wounds only. Bye Lester." She gave the bow a hard shove and turned and walked up the beach.

Lester pulled the starter rope, and the engine caught immediately. It almost always did. It was an Evinrude. It was the most reliable engine he had ever owned. It started easy and ran smooth at all speeds. As he moved out into the deep water, the engine purred like a cat, like the big tom that slept at the foot of Lester's bed. It was a very soothing sound, like music to his ears. Sometimes he thought it was the only music he would ever understand.

Arrowheads

Even as an adolescent, Roy still liked looking for arrowheads. In the spring the best places for finding them were the bare fields before they were plowed, but in the summer it was the bayshore. The best part of the bayshore was its southern tip where the beach ended among the marshlands of Barnacle Creek. Here, far away from houses, roads, cars, and people, Roy would wade for hours in the tidal pools formed by the tussocks of stubble, where the marsh itself was being washed away. The shallow pools acted like miners' pans and collected a sediment of bark, pebbles, broken glass, shells, and stones.

You almost never saw the entire arrowhead. You

had to look for clues: a corner, a tip, a certain color or texture of stone — scalloped edges of a piece of chert, the corrugated surfaces of milky quartz — that told you it was not bark, not shell, not ordinary stone, but worked rock. Only then would you pick it up. Even then you were usually wrong. Black chert turned into bark, crumbled in your hand; white quartz became an oyster shell; the grey finely grained stone, a certain spearhead, was a barnacle streaked with mud. But every now and then a tip would be exactly that; you'd flip it with your finger and feel the resistance of the rest of the stone sunk in the mud. That instant of recognition, of discovery, never stopped exciting Roy.

The first thing he would do with every find was wash it off. The second was admire the stone. He knew the names, dates, uses of the various styles of arrowheads. He even knew that "arrowhead" was not the right name. "Projectile point" was what they should be called, but who cared? Analysis was for later. The bayshore at Barnacle Creek was not a place for science. It was wild and uninhabited, and, except for erosion, it probably hadn't changed in hundreds or thousands of years. It was place to forget what you had learned from books, and to let your imagination run wild. Sometimes Roy would hold an arrowhead in his hand and shut his eyes and see what images played across his mind, and wonder what hands had held that stone before his, and what or whom had those hands touched?

Searching the shallow pools almost hypnotized Roy, and he would lose all track of time except that told by the tide and sun. No point looking when the tide reached a certain height or the sun the wrong angle. Then he would sit on the beach for a while and enjoy the solitude. He almost never saw another soul on that section of beach. Even a footprint was a mystery: a crabber in search of washed up buoys? A trap fisherman after stakes? To see an actual person was a shock. And one day to see a woman in a two piece bathing suit — at first he thought his eyes had lied to him. He thought his fantasies, which weren't always about Indians, had gotten the best of him.

Then, as the woman came closer, he recognized her. It was his cousin, Evelyn Harmon Hoyt. He felt embarrassed because, even though he still liked looking for arrowheads, he thought of it as a childish pursuit, something he probably should have outgrown and just hadn't quite yet. And because Evelyn in the past had always treated him like a child, and he didn't want her to. He stood up, brushed the sand off his bathing suit and sauntered over to her, to let her see how tall he'd gotten.

She took off her dark glasses and squinted at him. "Roy?" she said. "I heard you were down, but I still hardly recognized you. You're all grown up."

He shrugged. This was a little more like it. "What brings you all the way down to this end of the beach?" Roy asked.

"I felt like walking. Felt like being alone. Lester dropped me on the sand point. I helped him fish his gill net?"

"Oh, yeah? How'd he do." Roy didn't go out with Lester now that he had sold the big boat.

"All right, I guess. A couple of bushels. He seemed satisfied."

"What were they?"

"I don't remember. Trout, spot, crabs, sea nettles, who knows?" She didn't seem to want to talk about fish. She held out her hurt hand. "Look what happened to me," she said. There was a cut on her thumb. "A big Jimmy crab."

"You're not supposed to pick them up by their claws," Roy said.

"Very funny. You sound just like Lester, you know?"

Roy took it as a compliment, though it didn't sound like she meant it as one.

"Is my eye still red?" Evelyn said, leaning towards Roy.

"A little," Roy said. Evelyn smelled like suntan lotion and perfume and maybe hairspray. He couldn't separate all the aromas, but they were different from anything he had ever smelled before, more exotic, and exciting.

"Sea nettle juice," she said moving away, rubbing her eye again.

"I know that does hurt," Roy said. "Let me look at that again."

She leaned back towards him and he took a closer look at her eye. Her closeness, the sweet aroma of the lotion and the hot sun had a strange effect on Roy. He felt kind of woozy, in a pleasant way, as if he'd had a beer or two. "Yeah, he got you all right," he said.

She moved back, removed a small makeup kit from her beach bag, checked herself in the mirror, first the eyes then her hair. A few wet curls were plastered to her forehead by perspiration. "I look like a wreck," she said.

"You look fine," Roy said. He meant it. He liked

how she looked. She looked more sophisticated than the girls he knew. Part of it may have been her reputation within the family. Evelyn was mysterious and worldly. Roy didn't know the specifics. He'd always been considered "too young" to know. So what Roy imagined was probably much worse than what he hadn't been told. All he knew for sure was, she'd been married more than once and owned a restaurant in Baltimore.

When Evelyn finished tidying up her face and hair, she closed the compact with a sharp snap. "So, anyway," Evelyn said, "what are you doing all the way down here by yourself?"

"Just walking," Roy said, "and looking to see if anything of interest had washed up on the beach since I was here last."

Evelyn smiled. "You too, huh? Find anything?"

"A few arrowheads," he said casually as if he'd just happened upon them.

"Oh, neat. Can I see them?"

Roy reached into the pocket of his bathing suit and showed her what he'd found, four arrowheads. Two were broken at the tip; another was intact but fairly ordinary, but the fourth was the finest arrowhead Roy had ever found, ever seen. It was formed from two different shades of chert; the base was chestnut brown; the tip was cream. The two shades met in the center of the stone at a sharp angle, the same angle as that formed by the tip of the arrowhead.

Evelyn's fingers went straight to that stone. "It's beautiful," she said. "It's a work of art. I had no idea the Indians did that sort of work."

"Most people don't," Roy said.

Then Evelyn held the arrowhead, tip down, against her chest. "It would make a beautiful pendant." She looked up and batted her eyes at Roy. "I don't suppose you'd consider..."

Roy sighed and shifted his feet. "I'd rather not part with that one," he said, deepening his voiced, hoping to sound detached and scientific. "This one is of considerable archeological interest. I'm sort of a collector."

Evelyn sagged and tucked the stone back into his pocket. "O.K.," she said, sounding like a disappointed little girl.

"I'll tell you what," Roy said. "I'll show you where to find one on your own. It would mean more to you if you found your own."

She brightened. "Will you help me look?"

Roy hesitated, "I promised Lester I'd help him pull his skiff up when the tide was high enough. It needs to be caulked and re-coppered." Evelyn made a sad face. "But I'll help get you started," Roy added. "O.K.?"

"I guess," she said without much enthusiasm. She set her beach bag on the sand and followed Roy down to the tussocks and tidal pools. "It's mud!" she said.

"No, it isn't. It's just a different texture of sand."

"It feels like mud."

"It comes right off. It won't hurt you. Come on." He took her hand and led her through the tidal pools. He told her what to look for, the tips and edges, the texture of rock. "You almost never see the whole arrowhead." He told her to try and ignore the shells, sticks, pebbles and other debris, but he had a hard time following his own advice, because every time Evelyn leaned over to examine a piece of bark or shell

Roy could see down the front of her bathing suit. He began having mixed feelings about wanting her to find an arrowhead. Soon he heard himself encouraging her to examine what were obviously not arrowheads, just so she would lean over. He wasn't terribly proud of himself, but he wasn't ashamed either. Somehow in this remote place, where there was more evidence of primitive man than of so-called civilization, it seemed O.K. to let your instincts loose.

But after a while he realized that no matter how far she leaned over, there was only so much he could see. Besides she was his cousin. Also the tide was rising, and there was Lester to think of. After twenty minutes of looking, Evelyn didn't seem any closer to finding an arrowhead than when she'd begun. Finally Roy reached into his pocket and found his second best arrowhead, and when Evelyn wasn't looking, tossed it out in front of her. Then he guided her towards it. Even then she could not seem to see it. Even though it was lying there fully exposed. Finally he pointed it out to her. "What's that over there?" he said. "Probably just an oyster shell, but you might as well check it out."

She leaned over and picked it up. "No," she said without much excitement, "it is an arrowhead. But not a very good one." Then she turned and slung it out into the bay. It skipped once and sank.

"What the are you doing!?" Roy said.

She turned and looked him squarely in the eye. "I'm teaching you a lesson, young man, one that will be very valuable to you in later life: Never treat a woman like a child, even if she's acting childish. Especially if she's acting childish."

"O.K.," Roy said. What else could he say? He didn't know how to talk to women.

"Of course, if it had been the pretty one," Evelyn said, "I would have kept it. That's the second lesson: every woman has her price."

Roy nodded. He felt like he was back in grade school. Who was he kidding anyway? Evelyn was out of his league. She was a woman of the world, and he'd only been out of Virginia a couple of times. "Well," he finally said, looking at his watch, "I guess I'd better be getting back."

"Would you like something to drink before you go? I've got a Coke in my bag. Don't know how cold it is."

"Sure," Roy said. "Why not?" It was hot, and he'd been out there a long time.

They walked back up to where she'd left her bag. He helped her spread her beach towel on the sand. When she opened the Coke, which had been in the sun, foam spurted from the top of the bottle. Evelyn held the bottle to her mouth until the foam settled. When she handed the bottle to Roy, she was laughing and her eyes were watering from the carbonation. Soda was running down her chest. "What a mess," she said.

The Coke was warm, but it still tasted good to Roy. Better than good, because the flavor of the soda was mixed with the taste of Evelyn's lipstick. In fact, it was the best Coke Roy had ever tasted; he knew he would remember it for a long time. When he handed it back to her, she smiled.

"You look like you just got kissed," she said.

"What?"

"You've got lipstick all over your mouth." She wiped

his lips with her thumb.

Even her thumb tasted good. "Well," Roy said, collecting himself. "It was nice seeing you again."

"Before you go, will you do me a favor," Evelyn said.

"What's that?"

She tossed him the tube of suntan lotion and lay face down on the towel. "Do my back," she said. "Please."

Roy looked at his watch, then down at Evelyn's back. How long could it take to do a back? "Sure," he said, kneeling down beside her on the towel. He squeezed some of the white lotion into the palm of his hand and sniffed it. Somehow it didn't smell the same in his hand as it did on her. It was nice, but it wasn't the same.

"Before you start," Evelyn said, "make sure you've got all the sand off your hands. That's very important."

"O.K.," he said, brushing the sand off on his bathing suit.

He started at the pale top part of her neck near the hairline and worked his way down to the base of her neck and out onto her shoulders. Her skin was surprisingly smooth and soft. He thought because it was already tan, it might be leathery and tough, but it wasn't at all. He re-lathered his hands and covered her shoulder blades and upper spine. She wriggled her upper back the way his cat sometimes did when he rubbed her. "You didn't tell me you were an expert," Evelyn said.

"I'm not," Roy said.

"Such sensitive hands."

He got more lotion and moved down to the middle

and lower portions of her back.

"Wait," she said.

Roy flinched. He thought maybe he had gone too far, or she had read his mind, but that wasn't it. She reached back with both hands and deftly undid the top of her bathing suit, and pulled the loose ends down out of the way.

"Mustn't have any lines," Evelyn said. "I like a nice even tan."

"Right," Roy said.

Now her whole back was exposed. Except for the skimpy bottom to her bathing suit, it was as if she were naked. "Forget about that," Roy told himself. "Concentrate on the job." He tried to approach her lower back the same as if he had been caulking and coppering the bottom of a skiff. You had to make sure every inch was covered, every nook and cranny, the furrows between her ribs, the low places between the ridges of her spine, all of it.

He caught a glimpse of his watch, glanced over at the tide, and remembered his promise to Lester. If he left now, he'd probably still be too late to pull the skiff up. Then neither job would get done right. And wasn't Evelyn a relative too? Wasn't she entitled to the same courtesy and consideration as Lester? Of course, she was.

"Want me to do the legs?" Roy blurted, sounding, he hoped, like a young professional, a handyman or maybe a house painter.

"Ahm, sure," Evelyn said, "if you'd like."

"No problem," Roy said, turning the other way on the towel.

The supply of lotion was dangerously low. He rolled

the tube from the bottom the way you would a tube of toothpaste. If he had to, he'd borrow lotion from her back. He'd used enough there. Her back was shining like polished copper.

He started with the soles of her feet — burned soles could be very painful — and worked quickly up to her ankles and then her calves. Her calves were strong and muscular, like a boy's only nicer, smoother, and no hair except a fine stubble that reminded him of how the marsh grass felt to the bottoms of his feet. He shut his eyes and imagined he was wandering back among the tidal pools looking for arrowheads. Soon he found himself at the soft places behind her knees, and then he was above her knees in new and unfamiliar territory, where the hair was no longer shaved. It was the farthest he'd ever been with a woman, and even if he'd got there under false pretenses, and even if she was his cousin, it still counted.

His fingers moved tentatively along until he felt Evelyn take his wrists affectionately but firmly in her grasp. He felt disappointed and relieved at the same time. He withdrew his hands and helped her fix the top of her bathing suit, because she was having trouble doing it alone. Without looking at him, Evelyn sat up and groped around in her beach bag until she found her cigarettes. Her hands were shaking. "You don't smoke yet, do you." Her voice was shaky too.

"No," Roy said. "Thanks anyway."

She sat with her arms wrapped around her knees; she still wouldn't look at him. "What about that skiff?" she said. "I thought you had some work to do." Then Roy realized she was crying.

"Look," Roy said, "I'm sorry if I upset you."

She turned towards him. Her eyes were red and filled with tears, but she was smiling. "No, no, no," she said. "Don't apologize. You did fine. You were sweet and kind and a little horny, sure, but so what? You're supposed to be at your age, and I encouraged it, but that's not the point. It's the other that threw me."

"I don't get it."

"I'm sure you don't." She inhaled and sighed. "See — and don't take this personally, but I operate under the principle that all men are bastards. They're born that way; they'll always be that way, and I let it go at that. It's neat, clean, and it's not all that inaccurate. And then to be reminded that men too — men! — start off in such a state of innocence — it just hurts. That's all. It's easier the other way. Safer." She inhaled, then flicked her cigarette towards the water.

"Innocence?" Roy said. He certainly didn't feel innocent. He'd lied to his uncle and practically raped his cousin.

"Relatively speaking. Relative to what comes later."

"And where'd you get the idea that all men are bastards anyway?" Roy said.

"Where do you think?"

"I don't know."

"Oh, Roy," she said, "you are sweet." She leaned over and rested her head on his shoulder and draped an arm across his knees. "I just wish the rest of the world could be like this farm, this beach. Don't you?"

"That would be nice," Roy said, but he didn't realize then that farm was so different from the rest of the world. He would always remember that this was where he heard it first and that it was Evelyn who told him. And even though she made it sound like common knowledge, it felt like she'd confided in him. He put his arm around her shoulders and rested his head against hers. They sat like that for a long time, neither of them talking.

When it finally really was time for Roy to leave, he stood up, reached into his pocket, and removed the arrowhead, the one he knew she wanted. She folded his fingers around it and squeezed his fist. "But I want you to have it," he said. "I do."

"I know you do, and I accept it. In fact, I insist on having it. But, I want it to remain in your collection for safekeeping. A stone of such 'archeological interest' shouldn't be separated from the others. You can label it, 'On loan from Evelyn Harmon Hoyt.'"

"O.K.," Roy said. What else could he say? It was the perfect solution. "You're pretty smart, aren't you?"

She laughed. "Oh, brother."

The way she said goodbye with a warm hug, a kiss on the cheek, then a quick friendly one on the lips, was more like she was saying goodbye, not to her little cousin, but to one of her men. Roy liked that very much, and when he got home, he labeled the arrowhead exactly according to her request.

126